MY LIFE
Interpreted

HOW I DISCOVERED THE KEYS TO FULFILLMENT WITHIN MY EVERYDAY EXPERIENCES

WANDA OCTAVE

Published by Wonderlife books
Printed in the USA

ISBN: 9769555711
ISBN 13: 9789769555716

This book is dedicated to:

Everyone who has ever questioned
the meaning of life -
The answers are right in front of you.

Life is short...
Always leave an
impression

Mianda

Introduction

For more than twelve years, I had been sharing (via e-mail) weekly messages, which I called *meditations,* to my close friends and family. After much persuasion and to honor a deep cry from within my soul, I put together a collection of my favorite reflections which birthed this book.

I call these meditations because I believe that if you meditate and by this I mean pause and think deeply about the meaning of the messages, you can expand the scope of your awareness. Intended to be read as a daily meditation for ninety-nine days, each life lesson or observation will encourage you to take a closer look at your circumstances and empower you to make decisions that serve your happiness and bring you peace.

All the stories you will read are true and based on my personal experience, though some names may have been changed or omitted for privacy. At the end of each meditation, you will be given a new instruction—another reason to express your creativity and nurture your authentic self.

Life is short…and it is constantly speaking to you. Listen.

#1
Be Aware of the Skeptics

Whatever your goal in life, you have to believe in yourself. Conviction, confidence, and determination, I believe, are the most powerful prerequisites to success. Know what you want to achieve. Believe in it, sell it, live it, honor it, be it! And stick with it—no matter what. You have to be in it for the long haul. Most times you have to be your loudest cheerleader. You have to scream so loud that you drown out the noise of the skeptics. Fulfill your destiny regardless of *the odds, the statistics,* or *what has happened historically.* Remember that everything in life is not as it seems and your expression of your authentic self is what really matters.

Good and sensible advice should be heeded and thoughtfulness in decision making is warranted. However, be aware that some people are so skeptical about success that failure becomes their default experience. They intentionally or unintentionally project their negativity onto your dreams. Be confident in who you are before accepting advice. Though it is recommended that you evaluate many opinions before establishing one of your own, remember to listen to that still small voice inside. It's your soul telling you exactly what it wants to experience. Go for it!

I remember that just before I got married, I was surprised at how negative people were. Instead of their advice being objective, it seemed discouraging. I met a woman who asked me, "Are you sure you want to get married? Do you know that one in two marriages fail?"

"Yes," I said, "I've heard that one in two succeed!"

She was not amused. She shook her head. "You're young. You young people always believe that yours will be the one that works out."

"Thank God for that!" I said. "Otherwise the statistics would be worse!"

"Humph!" she said. "You think marriage is easy? Wait untill you have kids."

"I already do!" I said, still smiling.

I know the woman was thoroughly annoyed and believed that I was blinded by my *youth* and the fantasy of marriage. She never took the time to ask me about myself, my husband, or my expectations. She had no idea how old I was, how mature or immature I was or what my perceptions were. She just wanted to let me know that I had a one-in-two chance of failure. Not success—failure! Lucky for me, regardless of the "odds," marriage was an experience I wanted to have.

But whether it be marriage, career, or any other lifestyle choice, be alert enough to recognize the cynics, smart enough to heed advice, and courageous enough to dive in.

Life is short...cheer yourself on!

#2
Connect with Your Passion

I just watched two episodes of *Chefography* on the Food Network, a show that profiles famous chefs and Food Network personalities. Though the two chefs featured in these episodes, Paula Dean and Bobby Flay, were very different, they were both driven by the same thing: their love for food and their passion for cooking.

Or so it seemed…

After the shows, I kept remembering how exited both Paula and Bobby were when they realized that people loved their cooking. Could it be that their real passion was not food at all, but the desire to bring people joy through their cooking? Paula wanted to make people feel like they were in their mother's kitchen. She felt that when people ate out, they should feel like they were sitting at home. Bobby's desire was to educate people about the flavors and variety of food. He wanted to introduce them to different food combinations and cooking styles.

For both of them, their passion was connecting with people. For it is only when we truly connect with someone through our talent that we have really used it. When we use our talents specifically to fulfill the need in someone else's life, it drives us to create more. We feel a greater desire to use our gift because we see that it benefits another. It creates *passion*. It is this connection that confirms that we are living our life's purpose. We are touching/changing someone's life by doing what comes naturally to us.

I also believe that if reward is not our motivation and our primary reason for using our talent is to make someone feel good, say, giving them good comfort food, then they will remember that feeling longer than they will remember the food. Because it is our ability to give that *feeling*, that really sets us apart from everybody else—that is our real talent.

When your creativity touches someone enough to make them *feel*, you have made a connection. There are thousands of authors, but J. K. Rowling makes children feel magical. That's what they buy. Not her actual books, but the *feeling* they know they will get from reading them.

I believe that those who have not connected with their passion in life are missing out on true happiness and connection with people. Right now I think of you reading this. I know that I am connecting with you. You read these messages because they make you *feel* enlightened, understood, comforted, or centered. I am writing this because I want to share my experiences and connect with you. I feel like we are having a conversation.

Life is short...connect with your passion.

#3

What's Your Story?

Do you have frequent candid conversations with your children, your spouse, your friends, or your colleagues about your life? Do these people know who you really are, what it was like for you growing up, your childhood experiences, your lifelong dreams and deepest passions?

Or is it safer for you that they don't know? Are you so ashamed of your real self that you do not want to reveal it? Is it safer to pretend or show different sides of yourself to different people? Are any of these 'sides' even authentic?

The thing is, when you reveal your authentic self to others, not only will they understand you better, but that revelation will create a more meaningful and insightful relationship. And if it does not, then perhaps this is not a relationship that you are meant to continue.

Of course you should exercise judgment regarding who, when and what you reveal. Recognize that *being* yourself is not the same are sharing your personal information.

In the film *The Curious Case of Benjamin Button*, Daisy's daughter Caroline, finds out about her mom's extraordinary life by reading Benjamin Button's diary. A complete stranger enjoyed a fascinating life before becoming the "mother" that Caroline had known all her life. Isn't it a pity that our spouses and children don't know who we really are? Do we really want them to find out about our lives from anyone but ourselves?

We are so fascinated by the lives of the characters that we read in books and see on film, yet we are no different. We all have a story. What's yours?

Life is short…someone's waiting to hear your story. Do tell!

#4

Ancestry

I stood at my grandmother's funeral in 2006 and realized with shock that I was actually related to about three hundred of the five hundred people at the funeral. My grandmother lived for 102 years. She had eight children, my dad being the last. There were more than forty grandchildren, more than eighty-five great grandchildren, at least twenty-five great, great grandkids, and two great, great, great grandchildren whom I knew of. Looking around, I began to feel dizzy. How could I be related to all these people? But more importantly, all these people were here because of one woman. If it weren't for her, none of us would have been born. (Well perhaps our souls would have been here but not the distinct personalities that we know today.) Irene Serieux was actually responsible for a whole generation.

I am sure my grandmother never dreamed that she would create such a legacy. It was like a movie that opens with one woman, and by the end of the film, she has created a whole village of people, each with his or her own talents, dreams and ambitions. The energy of all these people contributes to the collective energy of the universe. My grandmother never realized it, but she was a force!

And so are you. You have no clue what your life's purpose is, really. Aside from your immediate contributions to society and your desire to be your authentic self, your life means so much more than you may get a chance to discover in this lifetime. Your life is connected to those who came before you and those who will follow. You are not only creating a life for yourself now, you are a source of influence far greater than you can imagine. You are creating a legacy that future generations will want to know about, talk about, learn from, and eventually embrace.

You know, some people leave their mark on the world, but there are those who actually change it. I am not sure what my grandmother's individual mark was, but with three hundred imprints (and counting), it's easy to see how one person can change the world!

Life is short...you are a connecting dot from one life to another. It is important that you understand that. Make this loop count!

#5
Tangible Format

I watched Lionel Richie tracking his ancestry some time ago, and as he held the only photo of one of his ancestors, I was reminded of how few actual photos I have of myself. What will my descendants find when they search for me?

I remember being so excited to see old photos of my mom, aunts, and uncles. The images not only captured their youth and innocence, but also hobbies, achievements, and their love for family. Spread across my living room floor was a tangible story. I could look, touch, and instantly connect. I did not need to wait for a VCR to play a tape, fret over scratches on a DVD, or worry about converting a file into a viewable format. A picture does tell a thousand words.

My mom went through great expense to restore, make copies of, and convert several old family photos in an effort to preserve her family history. She has also been scrambling to convert old cassettes to mp4 format and to find a record player for her old 45s. Technology is progressing so rapidly that we are losing the tangible formats of our most valuable memories.

Not too long ago, Neale Donald Walsch (bestselling author of the *Conversations with God* series) advised authors that while e-books may be trending, it is still advisable to get their books in print, as a hundred years from now, the physical book will still be accessible for anyone to read.

And while you can still enjoy the pleasure of reading with an e-reader, you can't deny the tease of an actual novel. When a good book sits on your nightstand, it stares up at you like a puppy waiting for a walk. It begs to be picked up. It is a glaring reminder of the pleasure of escape.

Technology is engrained into the fabric of all our lives these days. We have no choice but to embrace it and keep up with it. But as you do, recognize that the pace of your life has changed. Things are quicker so you move faster—so fast that you forget to stop to *take* a picture, or *print* that picture. You don't *pick up* a book anymore, or walk to your neighbor's. You don't even speak to your friends anymore, e-mailing or instant messaging instead. Haven't you realized that your fingers say a lot more than your mouth does these days?

Take a step back. Unplug. Who are you without your cell phone, laptop, or tablet? Can you pick up a landline and make a good ole fashioned phone call? How about meeting up with a friend for a real-life chat? Are you still able to connect?

Electronic formats will come and go, but nothing will ever replace something or someone that you can touch, feel, and enjoy the energy of.

Life is short...Leave a tangible trail.

#6
Success-full?

I like reading stories of people—biographies and autobiographies of famous people and articles about 'ordinary' people. So I didn't hesitate to pick up a magazine at the supermarket last week that promised "Amazing Stories of Successful Women." I began to flip through. All the women featured were incredibly accomplished and did seem to have gone through several obstacles and harrowing odds before they finally achieved the coveted life that so many crave. I noted, however, that there were no housewives, no public servants, or any other seemingly *ordinary* people on the list. All of the women featured were business owners and/or high-powered executives.

I gently put down the magazine and began to slowly push my trolley away. By these standards, I could be perceived a failure. So could my mom, my dad, the single mothers who raise college graduates, the friendly taxi driver who's in love with his city, the teachers who prepare our children for the future, the musician who sings his heart out at a restaurant every night, and the woman who sells food from a mobile truck because she would rather cook her heart out than sell her soul to a government cubicle.

What about those who do what they love every day—whether they face incredible odds or not?

Despite what the media says, success does not equal career woman or business tycoon. It has little to do with notoriety or the size of your bank account. Success is self-actualization – the personal fulfillment and contentment found when living a life of passion and purpose. So if being a career woman brings you that deep level of joy, then by all means strive for it. But if staying home and taking care of your family or fixing a car engine does, then dare to be yourself—strive for that! Success is staying true to who you are and being satisfied that you have done your best at it. Achieving notoriety is a bonus.

If you're still trying to figure out who you are, that doesn't mean that you're a failure. Be gentle with yourself. You are being prepared.

Life is short…believe in yourself. Step out into your very own spotlight.

#7

A Pinch of Salt

Some time ago I caught a persistent cold. As I pulled into my driveway after work, all I could think of was getting to the bathroom so I could gargle some warm salt water to get rid of my sore throat. Before I even put my bag down, I ran into the kitchen and grabbed the salt, only to realize that it was empty! I couldn't even scream. My voice was gone. Bridging on tears, I hoped that a painkiller would be enough to knock me out for the night.

Later, as I settled into bed, I wondered if I'd ever fall asleep because my throat hurt so much that I could hardly swallow. My mind began to drift to how financially strapped I was, and I felt an urge to search the pockets of my jeans and purses for any hidden cash, hoping to take the focus off the sharp knife in my throat. As I searched my work bag, I began to pray, "Lord, you know how hard things are; please make me find some hidden stash." At that precise moment, my hand touched something in one of the hidden crevices of my bag. I pulled it out in anticipation...it was a sachet of salt! I stared at the salt in disbelief. Then I threw my head back in laughter.

Perhaps no one ever told you, but God, He's a funny guy! He knew that my bills were paid, that I had food in my cupboard and petrol in my car. I did not need money. All I needed was that sachet of salt to cure my sore throat. He used my current desires to lead me to what I actually needed. And of course, it worked. I gargled away and slept like a baby.

Life is short...pay less attention to what you think you need and have faith that your needs will be met.

#8

Humor Me!

When I rent movies, I almost always rent a comedy. Comedies immediately relax you. They transport you to a world of fun. Their goal is to make you laugh, and a good one is guaranteed to keep you giggling and in high spirits for hours! Whoever said that laughter was the best medicine was spot on! Laughter relaxes and instantly changes your mood. It is absolutely essential in maintaining calm and peace of mind.

If you incorporate some form of comedy into your morning, or open yourself to receiving humor, you will find yourself laughing more throughout the day. You will feel much lighter!

In the evening after settling down, look for something funny on television. A few months ago, I watched Wanda Sykes's *I'ma Be Me* stand-up special, and I've been hooked ever since. The jokes kept me laughing for days. From then, stand-up became my new 'thing.' Instead of watching TV on an evening, I am now much more inclined to search YouTube for some of the good old favorites: Chris Rock, Wanda Sykes, Sinbad, Steve Harvey, best of BET Comic View, Dave Chapelle, and others.

You may have your favorites. Download them, rent them, watch them! Or read a funny book. Hook up with friends who make you laugh. I have an old friend whom I call every couple of months and we giggle on the phone for about an hour, just as we did when we were twelve. I always feel like a kid afterwards.

But whether it's a person, a standup routine, a joke, a TV show, a movie, or a book, you should find some way to incorporate humor into your life. It's the best stress reliever!

Life is short…laugh it off!

#9
Your Heart's Reflections

I introduced my daughter to an old friend recently, and as they chatted, my friend threw her head back in laughter. "My gosh, Wanda, you have made a miniature you! I remember when I first met you, I thought, 'Oh no, she is a miniature Emma,' and now, you have reproduced yourself!" She shook her head and laughed. "Three generations of high-spirited craziness!"

I chuckled and brushed it off, but it weighed on my mind. It was strange to be compared to my mother and my daughter all at once. My daughter has the same spunk, openness, and hunger for insight that I do, but I see none of these in my mom. While I know that my mom and I are alike in many ways and I actually feel proud when people make reference to it, I never got to experience her as an adult, or free spirit, the way I have been open enough to allow my daughter to see me.

I understand that my mother grew up in a world different from mine and that she prepared me for today as best as she could. As I mature, I realize that I am doing a lot of the things that she always wanted to do but for one reason or another was not able to. I think she knows that I have learned from her mistakes and admires the fact that I am not afraid to express my true self. I'd like to think that she is proud of the woman I've become. I am in part an expression of her in this time period.

Likewise, I am growing increasingly proud of and mesmerized by my daughter. She is only nine but is already so much wiser and more focused than many twenty-somethings I know. She is definitely a grander version of myself. I want her to be grounded in spirituality and start living authentically even at nine.

Have you ever noticed that the people around you reflect various aspects of yourself? Not only your children, but friends, family, and colleagues sometimes achieve things or do things that you always wanted to. You then go through the experience with them and get to enjoy it as well. Some live out your alter ego and you get to be part of it. You are constantly attracting the life you want, whether it is through you or through others.

In the song "In the Ones You Love," Diana Ross articulates it best.

"…May every wish and every prayer find its way, always be heard,
And every day, may you see them answered
In the ones you love, in the ones who love you.
Your heart's reflections come shining through,
Brighter than the sun, stronger than you knew,
In the ones you love, in the ones who love you"

Life is short…look around you. Your dreams are being fulfilled every day.

#10
A Mother's Day Story

I found myself very present on Mother's Day. I made a special effort to absorb, appreciate, and participate in all aspects of motherhood. And by the end of it, I actually felt very connected to my daughter and began appreciating and admiring little things about her. I was thankful for her giving spirit, her eagerness to help, and her constant need to express herself—to create something new. I was present. And so was she. It was evident that there was an actual chemistry between us, a cohesiveness.

She wanted me to enjoy the day. She made a special effort to be obedient, helpful, and loving. And when it was all over, we sat on her bed and she asked me grown-up questions about myself – She wanted to know the story of the day she was born, why I decided to get married and why I didn't want to have any more children. It was a sweet exchange that touched my soul.

I went to bed that night proud—proud of her and myself. She is an amazing person, and she is much more like me than I care to admit.

The next morning, as soon as she got out of bed, she said, "Mummy, can it be Mother's Day for the rest of the year?" Clearly, I was not the only one who felt the connection!

"Well, will you be helpful and totally obedient for the whole year?" She thought for a moment…

"OK, then, can it be Mother's Day twenty-nine days a month?"

"Why Kelci, so you can have a day or two to be naughty?"

"Well you can't expect me to be good *all* the time, Mummy. I'm a kid!"

And so ended my Mother's Day bliss. Less than an hour later, my regular morning yells began, forcing me to seek calm. I had to remind myself that it was OK to be in love with my child one day and want to beat some sense into her the next. Last week, a friend admitted that she had to drink three glasses of wine to calm herself down after her two-year-old and four-month-old kids finally fell asleep. She knew that there may be traces of alcohol in her breast milk, but for one night, she just needed to stay sane and sleep through. Then the day after, overcome with guilt about what she had done, she called me for counseling.

In trying to put my disciplinary challenges with my daughter and my friend's confession in perspective, I took a moment that day to reflect on the kind of daughter I'd been and what I may have driven my own mother to. I realized that we grow up and look back on our unruly or rebellious behavior and wonder how our parents survived us! But in the end, especially if the general environment was a loving one, every experience, good or bad, usually evokes a memory that we can bond with our parents over, talk about, or learn from when we have our own kids.

Life is short…every minute of your life is a memory created. Enjoy it.

#11

Adjectives

Recently, my mom asked me to describe each of my brothers and sisters using one adjective. There are nine of us, so I slowly went through the list, in some cases using nouns as I struggled to find adequate adjectives. Summing up someone I'd known practically my whole life into one word on the spur of the moment was a bit daunting, confusing, and unfair! With a person's complex personalities, behaviors, and emotions, I needed at least a five-word allowance to capture their essence, let alone a sibling. But I played along and as she named each one, I spat out my word.

Even though we have different relationships, I assumed that we had a fair understanding of one another and expected similar descriptions. It was very interesting and a bit shocking to learn what my siblings thought of me and of each other. Instead of a thesaurus, I was handed a workbook. I felt like my mom was stretching her hands out and saying, "Here is your family. Here is what you think of them, here is what they think of you, and this is what they think of each other. Now, how can you use this information?"

I felt uneasy. I began to wonder if we siblings knew each other at all. The family members who knew me best described me as deep, spiritual, and carefree. Others described me as strange, arrogant, and cheap. In some cases, I understood why my actions would be interpreted as such, while in others I felt misunderstood. It was clear that there were a few sibling relationships that I needed to work on. Though we may not have been close, that was not what I wanted their perception of me to be.

For the most part, every one of us at least wants to be understood. And we also want to know that we matter, that our lives make a difference—to family, friends, or someone. We don't expect everyone to agree with our point of view, but we want to know that we connected. And whether they liked us or not, whatever they thought of us, we had an effect, we connected... we mattered.

Life is short...what's your adjective?

#12
One Love

When I was younger, I used to have secret thoughts of people whom I didn't like disappearing, banished to some place where I would be spared the displeasure of dealing with them. I thought that if they were not around, then the world would be a better place *for me.* Forget using these unpleasant experiences as spiritual lessons or actually learning to control my own emotions. I just wanted to "avoid loud and aggressive persons" because they were "vexations to the spirit"—my spirit. As expressed in 'The Desiderata'.

Then a couple of weeks ago, I was listening to an interview with one of Bob Marley's sons. He said that his father believed that there were no degrees of love—only "One Love." The same love that you have for your mother, you should have for a tree because we are all one.

Intellectually I understood this, but you'd have to be a monk to get to that state of mind. I pull the weeds out of my garden and squash the mosquitoes on my arm…not the same love I have for my mother…noooo!

The same love and respect I have for my mother, I have for the supermarket clerk or a vagrant. But perhaps I need to profess it more, try to live it, and totally embrace it. Based on Marley's perception of 'One Love', this would mean that I am an extension of you and you are an extension of me. How then could I possibly want to harm you? You are me manifesting differently. I fully understand that now.

So I have come to forgive myself for all the negative thoughts that I directed at various people from my past. The Bible says, "Do unto others as you would like done to you". I shudder to think of what I've done to myself!

Life is short…strive for One Love!

#13
Dust!

While I was still trying to embrace the "One Love" concept and figuring out the best way to deal with the "vexations to my spirit," a close friend explained that she views negative people as dust or ash. If someone offends her, she pictures them as a blob of dust and thinks to herself, "You can't hurt me. You're not as arrogant as you think; you are ash…dust! Just like me. We are both dust!" And she looks at the big blob of dust in front of her and smiles.

We see people as we are, not as they are; we judge things based on our beliefs. We compare people to ourselves. We see people as selfish only because we see ourselves as giving. Someone else may see them as perfectly normal because he or she may be just as selfish.

I truly believe that we are here to learn from each other. In whatever way you affect my life, you are contributing to it. You make me who I am. No one is better than the other. We are all equal. Dust!

Life is short…you are not your ego.

#14
Oneness

Shortly after I wrote the meditation "One Love," I began receiving e-mails from various subscriptions, and found myself in strange circumstances that somehow facilitated my experience of oneness. I know that subconsciously, my mind needed to understand what my soul already knew. Mind you, before this, I believed in connection: connection with the source and connection with people. My way of connecting with nature was simply through admiration. Nature is astoundingly beautiful. Unlike my connection with God or people, my connection with nature was infrequent and one sided; I only felt a connection when I thought nature was beautiful. Only rarely did I think of what it could teach me or how my actions harmed it. My focus was on the human experience. Nature was an accessory, a backdrop so to speak, something to facilitate my existence. To help with food, air, and sunshine, and to make me feel good from time to time.

Until the day that I understood Oneness—the fact that nature and I are not separate and that One Love should exist because a tree *is* in fact just as significant as a human being.

We rationalize that things are connected through visual or emotional attachment. If we don't *feel* a connection and we can't *see* one, then we assume that one does not exist. We *feel* a connection to humans and pets because we allow ourselves to. We have been socialized to. We see the tree growing out of the ground; therefore, it is connected to the ground. The environment, we have learned, is separate from us. We don't *feel* a connection to plants (partly because we have not been taught how to), and there is no physical string connecting us to the atmosphere or the ground, so we keep seeing ourselves as separate.

If you close your eyes for a moment and imagine the air as a physical cord, you will see that the trees connect to us through the air and we to them. If we imagine emotion as a string, we will see how much we caress or electrocute each other with every emotion. As we eat the foods from the soil and the flesh of animals for nutrients, we are continuing the process of life. We need each other for sustenance of life! We are all one. If there were no atmosphere, plants, animals, sun, or water, we would not exist as we know it.

Look around you: You are connected. Everything is in you and you are in everything.

Life is short…embrace it. All of it.

15
Hindsight

If I knew back then what I know now
If I understood the what, where, why, and how,
Now it's clear to me what I should have done,
'Cause my hindsight is 20/20 vision.

—George Benson

Would you change your life if you were given a chance to relive it? Do you have visions of a different you? If a genie came up to you today with a time capsule, what would you change?

For me, that answer would change on a daily basis. Yet I believe that even if we did change the circumstances in our lives, the lessons would be the same. We should therefore pay attention to our experiences because they facilitate our lessons.

I have grown to be grateful for my experiences and embrace where they lead me. I have no regrets. I used to say that I would not change my past if I had the power to because I have enjoyed my life, but I don't think so anymore. Without discrediting my experiences or dishonoring any family or friends, I think I would choose a different path. Not because I did not or do not enjoy this one—but why repeat it? I appreciate the value of experience and personal growth. I would love to know a different me, experience more of me.

The funny thing is, we choose the experiences that shape our lives every day. We may not be proud of our past decisions, but we were not as wise as we are now. And the beauty of life is that we get to create a new experience through our choices at any time.

Oprah says, "Live your life on purpose." I agree.

Life is short…enjoy every experience of it!

#16

Life!

Diary Entry, February 2009

There seems to be a wave of death sweeping the air. Over the past few weeks, two of my relatives have passed, and last week my husband's best man died in his sleep.

Every time someone close to us dies, it brings to light our own mortality. For the first few days or weeks, we reevaluate our lives, we appreciate our families, we do the things we enjoy, and we begin to take care of ourselves. *Life* matters. And then the vicious cycle begins again and we fall into the daily grind. It usually takes someone else dying to wake us up again.

Everyone has his own idea of what death is. Most of us fear it because we do not want to leave our loved ones behind. But the thing is, when a soul leaves this earth, his time here is over.

His contribution to this life as we know it has ceased. But ours is still needed. *Life* goes on for us. While we grieve, it is important to remember that. We need to appreciate the lessons that our departed loved ones taught us. Their lives, also gave ours meaning.

This life is as much about you as it is about all those you touch every day. Make an impression on the people you meet. We cannot exist without each other. Our lives are shaped by the energies that we come into contact with each day. We create each other's lives. Be aware of that. Embrace it, and make it a worthwhile experience for everyone.

One of the things I find the most fascinating about life is the sheer complexity of it: nature, people, events, and the process of life itself. If you take a step back to examine the sum of all the parts, you will have no choice but to be in awe of life, then be excited to play the game, dance the rhythm, solve the mystery, join the circle…live the life!

Today life goes on for me. I carry on as normal, grateful that I am alive. I am reminded of a signature I once carried at the bottom of my emails *"When I die, I want to die empty. I want to have squeezed all the joy and excitement out of life! I want to have given so much and have lived so much that there is nothing left."*

Life is short…live!

#17
Live Life on Purpose

I have a friend who openly admits that at this time in his life, it's all about creating an impression. He has several vehicles: a high-end one that he only uses to attend meetings with influential persons, a middle-income one for every day running around, and a low-end one that can be rented out or loaned to friends and family. He owns several pieces of property: one in a high-end neighborhood, one in an up-and-coming area, and a few others in the rural areas. He sees them as investments, but he also believes that it is important to have a presence in as many communities as possible and be known by persons in all classes of society. Future politician? Perhaps…but that's not the focus for now. It's all about creating an impression.

He owns—and I am not kidding—more than a hundred work shirts and ties. I dare not ask how many pairs of shoes.

He's not gay, neither is he conceited or flamboyant. In fact, he is one of the most down-to-earth people you will meet. And as crazy and over-indulgent as he is, he is one of the kindest and most genuine people I know. Without fail, he will go out of his way to help you. He is the guy that you call at 1:00 a.m. when you're stranded by the roadside. He will come. And if he is unable to, I am one hundred percent certain that he will find someone who will.

He is purposefully intense about everything he does. He lives his life on purpose. His personal life, his work, his investments, sports, social commitments—everything he does is calculated, meticulous, and done with the best intentions. His main priority is building and enjoying his life. He always remains true to who he is. He is aware. He is living! And I admire that.

I am not saying that we should all be that extreme. I sometimes wonder how he is able to keep up with his own life. But I wish we were all a little more aware—a bit more in tune with our lives, a bit more mindful of the repercussions of our actions, a bit more eager to help others, a bit more spontaneous—and that we could each be a more willing participant in our lives… just a bit more!

Life is short…live it on purpose.

#18

Don't Make Assumptions

"Don't Make Assumptions" is one of the Four Agreements discussed by New Age author Don Miguel Ruiz. Basically, this "agreement" states that you should find the courage to ask questions and express what you really feel. Communicate with others openly and clearly to avoid misunderstandings and unnecessary misinterpretations.

I have actually made this one of my resolutions this year, and there is a noted improvement in how I approach every situation. I do not presume to know someone else's response/reaction *before* I have actually spoken to him. I let things be and don't project any unnecessary worry. Everything just is, until I experience it.

We cannot presume to know how other people will respond to us. Usually, we project our feelings of how we *think* they will react and make decisions based on these assumptions. The actual outcome of any situation can be much different if we do not let the fear of a projected outcome consume us.

In the story "The Necklace" by Guy De Maupassant, a poor woman loses a necklace that she borrowed from her wealthy friend. She is so frightened about what her friend might do that she takes out a loan and replaces the lost necklace with a brand new one. For ten years, she works odd jobs and sacrifices many comforts to pay off the loan. Shortly after the loan is paid, she confesses to her friend what she has done, only to find out that the original necklace had been a fake. She had replaced a fake necklace with a real one only because she made assumptions about her friend's reaction. She had toiled unnecessarily for ten years of her life based on an assumption.

If we can overcome our fears of what we think people think of us and be brave enough to express ourselves, then we will accept any and every outcome. Our lives will be a more authentic expression of who we are. It will also give others a chance to be more open with us in return.

Life is short…don't make assumptions.

#19

When You're Standing at the Crossroads

Have you ever been faced with a difficult decision and had no clue what direction to take? You want to trust your instincts, but they tell you nothing. And you look high and low for signs, but there aren't any. Not even your gut has a reaction.

The thing is, we spend so much time focusing on the decision itself that we don't realize that the consequence of the decision is what we will really need guidance on. And though we may create little scenarios in our minds of what the long-term effects of our decision will be, we never really know for sure what the future holds.

So if it's too close to call, make the call anyway. Sometimes it is OK to make a decision without the help of counsel, instincts, or signs. We need to bite the bullet and trust that we will be strong enough to deal with whatever consequences and challenges that arise. We need to believe that we will receive the wisdom and counsel exactly when we need it in the (uncertain) future.

Life is short…when you're standing at the crossroads, don't hesitate—cross!

#20
Face the Consequences

So you stood at the crossroads and pondered your decision. Did you follow your gut? Did you make the decision based on what you wished to experience? Or were you blinded by the anticipated consequences of your decision?

More often than not, we get so caught up with the perceived consequences of our decisions that we fail to live our authentic lives. Again, we make assumptions on a future we are yet to experience. We don't do the things we love because we feel that our decisions will negatively affect our loved ones. We believe that they will *suffer* the consequences of our actions. Never mind the countless decisions we make every day. Conscious or unconscious, many of these have not-so-favorable effects on the lives of our loved ones or others anyway, even when we have the best of intentions.

Remember that this is *your* life. If you are not happy with where it is headed, then start making your own decisions. Because if you are not happy, you can be sure that this will bleed over into your relationships one way or the other, and your loved ones will suffer the unfavorable consequences of your unhappiness, in big or small ways.

Right now, I live life on purpose and make decisions based on the experiences I wish to have. Because I have a husband and child, I have to think of how my decisions will affect them, but I also remember that I am the only one who can live *my* life. If I want to have an authentic experience, I need to make decisions that make me happy. I encourage my family to do the same. I also pray that the critical choices that I make, are in the best interest of all involved. Being at peace with my decisions also helps me be at peace with the consequences.

I believe that if we really commit to living our authentic lives and embrace every experience, then every decision if done with the best intentions can only lead to enlightening consequences.

Life is short…are you ready to face the consequences?

#21
Burst That Bubble

A friend once told me that when something major is happening in her life, she finds it impossible to stop worrying. Her troubles keep following her throughout the day, popping up in her head like a cartoon bubble. I put my index finger close to her head, hit it with a quick jerk, and pursed my lips with a bubble-busting sound. "Pop that bubble," I said. "Stop and deal with it or it will keep showing up!"

There is an old saying that if the first thing you do in the morning is eat a live frog, nothing as bad can happen for the rest of the day. Motivational speaker and Business Consultant Brian Tracey used this as a basis for some of his books and lectures, and he refers to the frog as your most challenging task of the day. If every day you "eat your frog" first, then you are able to have more mental clarity to focus on other duties because, frankly, the worst is over.

If you do not deal with your frog, however, you will be unable to function effectively. In addition, like a nagging child, that frog, that bubble, will keep popping up for days, weeks, months… until you deal with it. Bite the bullet, eat that frog, burst the bubble, taste the discomfort, feel the embarrassment, and move on.

If you seek peace, you need to be free to make more rational decisions without having bubbles cloud your judgment.

Life is short…burst that bubble.

#22
A Magic Carpet Ride

One particular scene in Disney's *Aladdin* has stayed with me since I last saw it. After Aladdin first kisses the princess, he lets himself drop (backwards) off the balcony. He is so confident that the carpet will be there to catch him, he never gives a thought to falling down. He has unconditional trust in…*a carpet!*

Most of us don't even trust each other, yet we put our trust in things of limited value. We trust our cars to take us to work. We trust our money to grow and we trust our house to keep us safe. But you and I both know that cars break down, houses get broken into, and the stock market's bipolar.

The truth is, as difficult as it is to trust one another, we do it every day. If we trust our car, for example, we need to realize that we really trust the engineers, assemblers, and mechanics who did the safety checks on that car. We trust investors, stockbrokers, chefs, and the actual people behind the scenes in our lives every day.

Why then are so many of us so guarded? We don't believe in each other anymore. We don't open up or give others the opportunity to. So few of us can take that magic carpet ride. Can you imagine trusting someone so completely that whatever situation you find yourself in, you know for certain that they will be there to support you?

Do you have a magic carpet? A few trusted family members and friends whom you could fall back on if you were to drop?

Life is short…you need a safety net. Build one.

#23
What Hat?

I'm sure you've heard the saying "Don't hang your hat higher than you can reach." Or you may be familiar with the popular nineties track "Waterfalls" by TLC ("Don't go chasing waterfalls, please stick to the rivers and the lakes that you're used to...").

Some time ago I told someone that I wanted to retire within the next two years. She rolled her eyes with disgust, and then suddenly the daggers came from nowhere. "You're in your thirties, your home isn't finished, your daughter is under ten, you don't have enough money saved, the world is in recession—how could you possibly retire in two years? Why don't you want to work hard like everybody else? I don't know what is wrong with this new generation, always trying to hang their hat higher than they can reach!"

OK. I took a breath, paused, and shook off the negativity. Yes, she had just pissed all over my dreams. Another breath. Did she really believe that that little speech would stop me? Another breath. "You will prosper in the famine," I said to myself. I looked her dead in the eye and said confidently, "You'll see."

I went away from the conversation sad—sad that so many people impose their beliefs on our dreams. Aren't we *supposed* to dream? Aren't we supposed to have goals and ambitions higher than that of our parents' generation? How on earth would anyone have achieved greatness if we didn't? I have to hang my hat higher than I can reach or else I will never reach higher. Why should I just keep stretching up to where I think I can get to? Stars are born when ordinary people push beyond their limits. Breakthroughs are made when we conquer the seemingly impossible.

I will not stick to the rivers and the lakes that I am used to. I will chase the waterfall. I believe I can reach it. And if I don't, I still would have traveled a bit further, stretched a bit higher, and came one step closer. I would have achieved something greater than what was expected of me. I would have built on the legacy of my parents. I would have set a precedent for my children so that they too can now hang their hat a little bit or quite a bit higher than I did. I would have assisted in the progress of humanity.

So I say, "What hat?" or "What waterfall?" There are no limits. If you want something, go after it. Believe that you will receive it. Trust that everything in the universe is working for you to have it. And if you don't achieve it, appreciate the journey anyway. It has brought you one step closer to your goal. Perhaps not in the way that you hoped, but closer.

Life is short…chase those waterfalls baby!

#24
Pissed!

After I sent out the "What Hat?" meditation to my e-mail list, I received a phone call from a close friend who was clearly upset with the "tone" of my writing.

"Did you read it?" I asked.

"Yes, I read *'pissed'*!" she said.

"Huh?"

"'She pissed on my dreams'?" (I could picture her, rolling her eyes.)

"Oh," I said, "yeah, she did piss on my dreams." I laughed.

"Yes, Wanda, but you shouldn't say *'pissed.'* You could have found a better, less offensive way of saying it. You are in a position of influence. You have to watch your language. You don't find TD Jakes or Oprah speaking like that!"

"Perhaps not but I know others who would," I said, defending myself.

"In any event, if you want to aspire to anywhere greater, to release a book and have people respect you, you need to watch the tone of your writing. People will lose respect for you if you use that kind of language."

"What? So I can't say *'pissed'*?" By then I was beginning to get irritated and just wanted to hang up the phone.

"Look," I said, "it's not about putting on a show for anyone, and *trying* to be respectable. I am being myself. I'm sorry that a stupid little word like 'pissed' offended you so much. I hope you got the message anyway."

I left that conversation really *pissed*! Funny how someone can use one word to completely derail you. I am not trying to be Mother Theresa. "Pissed" is a verb (and an adjective). Yes, I could have said, "She spat on my dreams," and that would have had the same effect. But I did not feel spat on. I felt pissed on. So I expressed that. This is a platform to express my feelings. I don't want to feel confined to acting like a nun. I do understand that I have a responsibility to my readers but I'd also like to believe that they've come to know me and have grown with me. They value my honesty and know that I'm not perfect. Even though I try to be impeccable with my word, (in every sense of the word) my choice of language will not always be perfect. I am human.

I felt uneasy having to defend myself to my friend, although I understood that she represented the concerns of other readers who may be 'turned off' by such language. She may have understood the intended message of my meditation, but because she felt so strongly about the use of one word, her image of who she thought I should be, overshadowed the message itself.

It stung. I wished sometimes we would just lighten up a bit. Yes there is a place for quoting scripture but there are times when we need to recognize that what is taking place in the present moment is more important than being *spiritually* correct.

Pissed!

I remember Sarah Ban Breathnach telling Oprah that people had built up an image of the person who wrote *Simple Abundance*. They had so many expectations of that image. She was supposed to speak a certain way and dress a certain way, and she definitely should not have gotten divorced!

I keep shaking my head. There is no mold. We need to get to that place where we can appreciate the bigger picture. I think it is more important to look beyond the labels, social definitions, character, and language, and appreciate the lesson, the message...the journey.

Pissed, spat, killed, crushed—it's all language.

Life is short...express yourself!

#25
Your Opus

The movie documentary *The Opus* was not as popular as *The Secret*, but just as powerful. Oddly enough, I am more drawn to the message of *The Opus* as it focuses more on the self. On expressing who you are. On making a contribution that enhances the lives of others. On specifically using your gifts to transform those around you.

To quote from *The Opus*, "Life is about the difference you made while you were here and the legacy you leave behind. Your Opus isn't just what you do; it will be the legacy of what you have become."

There is only one of you, so your contribution matters. And according to psychologist Abraham Maslow's Hierarchy of Needs, you can only truly make that contribution after you have satisfied your basic needs for survival, safety, intimacy, and self-esteem. At that point your only desire is to express yourself. To "self-actualize". To live your dream. To *be* you.

I believe that self-actualization is a feeling, a feeling of knowing exactly who you are, where you are (in life), what you've learned, what your contribution means, and how much more you can give. Remember my earlier meditation, "Connect with Your Passion"? Your talent fulfills a need in other people. It makes them "*feel.*" And there's no greater joy (to both of you) than to feel a connection—to connect with your words, your music, your life. And when others feel you, they remember you, long after you've gone.

Maya Angelo famously said 'I have learned that people will forget what you said, people will forget what you did, but people will never forget how you made them feel'.

I believe that the only way to truly create a legacy is to live such an extraordinary or exemplary life that it cannot be forgotten. Leave your mark so that when you die, the essence of who you are keeps on living here on earth through those you've touched. You not only affect your generation, but you help build another.

Life is short…what's your opus?

#26
Pass It On

You have very few original thoughts. And these *original* thoughts are usually conceptualized based on your rationalization of what you learned in the past. Everything that you know now, you know because someone passed on an ancient or original thought. Learning equips us with the skills necessary to go through life.

So just as you have learned from your elders, you should pass on what you know. You are gifted with talents and ideas that can change the world. Find an outlet. Find a muse. Unleash your creativity. You may be the next Mozart, Bill Gates, or Martha Stewart.

Embrace the past. Learn from it and churn out modern ideas. Pass them on. New ideas create history.

To quote the multitalented writer Hope Clark, "Stay open to the past and the present, because it's only by knowing both that you can walk intelligently into the future."

Life is short…share your talents.

#27

Unclutter Your Life – Give

Helping someone does not always mean a financial handout. People need food, clothes, and so many things that we take for granted or waste every day. A book that you read five years ago is needed in someone's life today. You may have been keeping it because of its sentimental value, but perhaps it's time to let someone else in on the wonder. Pass it on. You can only use so many pots and pans or beauty products. Give them away. Think of the joy they will bring to others who truly need them.

I recently came across some picture frames and other household items that I had purchased on sale and tucked away but never used. I pushed them back into the cupboard and told myself that I would get them all out when I redecorated. But would I *really* use them then? I was not so sure. They might not match my theme or décor, or I may lose interest, or...

I decided to give them away. I also went from room to room searching for things that I no longer used, things that I had been saving for later and others that had lived out their usefulness.

I wondered - why do we horde things that mean nothing to us? Why do we buy impulsively or compulsively knowing that we already have enough? If we only used something once or twice, why keep it? Are we so selfish that we'd rather hold on to something we don't need just because we paid for it? Don't we realize that it is by uncluttering that we can make room for what we truly deserve?

If an item plays no role in your present life, brings no pleasure, *and* takes up space in your home, it's time to let it go. If you have not used it in more than six months, chances are you don't need it and may never use it. Going forward, try to resist the hot sales and treasured *finds* that you know you can do without. Also, it is a good idea to repeat your un-clutter exercise every six months or at least once a year. You will be amazed at what comes into your life to replace the 'clutter'; Bearing in mind that some of your new fortunes may not always be tangible.

Life is short…un-clutter your life. Give!

#28
Balance

Experts say that we need to find balance in our lives. I think that striving for balance will make us more stressed out than living our already hectic lifestyle. Even in an ideal world, a balanced life is not possible.

We have been socialized to believe that there are certain roles and responsibilities that we need to carry out as we become adults. Many of us become torn between performing traditionally expected roles, fulfilling social responsibilities, and following our passions. We think that a little bit of all three will keep us within the cookie-cutter definition of balance, so we exhaust ourselves to fit it all in.

But what if this "balance" still does not make us happy? Do we really need balance to be fulfilled? What if our mission in life is greater than the balance that we seek? Consider a father who spends little time with his family because he spends too much time at work, traveling the country building schools in under-privileged neighborhoods. He knows that he is not spending enough time with his family, but every time he cuts a new ribbon, he also knows that he is giving thousands of children the chance at an education and a better life. With all of his being, he *knows* that this is what he is meant to be doing with his life. And it is what makes him truly fulfilled even if it means spending less time at home.

It is nearly impossible to find balance and be effective in every area of your life. You can still enjoy a bit of everything, but you must know that one area will suffer while you truly commit to another. One day at a time, I try to enjoy my life with no regard for balance. I do what moves me when I feel like it and somehow it all gets covered. Sometimes, I am selfish and focus on my needs only. Other times, I take care of everyone else and neglect myself. Then there are times when I get absorbed in my work and only extreme hunger gets me out of the chair. Through all of this, I try to align myself with The Source—God. And I also know that the universe is completely balanced as it is. And that my unbalanced life contributes to the perfect, harmonious, balanced circle of life.

Life is short...Live in moderation.

#29
When You're Caught in Someone Else's Lesson

I had been waiting for a response from a potential employer that had me a little anxious. A favorable decision would mean sustained jobs for at least six people. If the decision was unfavorable, these persons faced a possibility of termination. I began to pray for the people who were about to make the decision that would affect my life and by extension the lives of others. I prayed that they would grant me favor over other applicants. I prayed for everyone else who would be impacted by the decision. I knew that some of them were not as calm and hopeful as I was, but I prayed that *they* be blessed with patience, calm, and a strong dose of optimism.

As I named each one, the focus and reason for my prayer changed. My prayers got deeper and longer than those that I had prayed for myself. My mind began to race. Why was I so concerned for everyone else? What was their role in all of this? Did they have a much deeper lesson to learn here than I did? What was my lesson? What was theirs? Why was I so calm? Why did my focus keep drifting back to praying for everyone else but myself? Was this about me at all?

In that moment, I recalled the movie *Saving Private Ryan*. Although saving Private Ryan was the objective, the movie was more about the journey of the soldiers who were deployed to save Ryan than about Ryan himself. The rescue mission was only the plot. Ryan was caught up in the other soldiers' lesson and he was totally unaware of their struggles.

It suddenly dawned on me that I may be caught up in someone else's lesson. I had no doubt that there was a lesson in there for me too and I would get to it. But as I stepped back and looked into the movie that was my current circumstances, I realized that this was not about me. I also realized that it was familiar. A bit too familiar. I had been there before…

Have you ever found yourself smack in the middle of a situation that you made every attempt to avoid? You were sure that you had learned your lesson the last time. You did everything right, yet the horrible situation seemed to repeat itself and you were left again to pick up the pieces.

I realized that the answers to the tragedies in our lives are found within the questions we ask while going through them. If you ask, "Why me? I have been through this several times before. I played by the rules; why on earth should I have to go through this all over again?"

The answer is: Because you have been through it before, because you have followed all the rules, because you *have* learned from the last time, and because this is a breeze for you. But this time, *it is not your lesson*. You needed to be there in the middle of it so you could be a blessing or a revelation to the person whom this is really about.

It took some time to absorb this, but accepting it, happened to be the actual lesson that I learnt.

It is never all about you. As you know, at any one time, there are many people affected by your actions or decisions. 'All the world's a stage, and all the men and women merely players' Shakespeare said. You may be in the movie, but don't kid yourself—you are not the star of every scene.

You need to pause and take a look at the bigger picture. Rick Warren, author of *The Purpose Driven Life*, said that "God's main focus is not to make us comfortable, but to build character." And I have learned that most times, we need to learn to make ourselves comfortable while God builds our character.

Next time you're faced with a challenge, or you find yourself in the middle of a crisis, look beyond yourself. All the world is indeed a stage, your lesson is just one scene, and that scene, part of a larger production. We're all in this together. It's not just about you!

Life is short…play your part.

#30

When You're Caught in Someone Else's Blessing

Just as you may be caught up in someone else's lesson, you can also be caught in someone else's blessing. But be prepared, 'cause the irony is that there will be a lesson in there for you too. You may have received a gift that you did not realize benefits someone around you more than it does yourself. While the spotlight may be on you, the real beneficiary may not be you! You may be so consumed with your 'prize' that you miss this lesson. Keep your eyes open. Recognize the ripple effect of everything that happens in your life.

Pay attention, too, when someone receives something that you have been wishing for. It may seem especially difficult if you feel that this person is not as deserving as you, or does not appreciate the gift as much as you would have. But before you get caught up in bitterness and envy, be grateful that you are actually part of that miracle. There is a reason why you are a witness to this. It is said that the best way to achieve success is to help others achieve it. Not only do you benefit from the experience, but you also attract more of that which you desire.

Life is short…count your blessings. You may be smack in the middle of one.

#39

When That Small Voice Is Screaming!

A few years ago, I was in agony. By all appearances, I had the perfect life. I was happily married, I had a wonderful daughter, a great job, made good money and was in perfect health. I also drove a nice car and built a beautiful home.

There was just one *major little* problem.

I was unhappy with the direction of my life. I yearned to do more. I yearned to *be* more. I wanted to write, to share my story, to share my thoughts, to connect with people. I knew that the small voice inside of me was screaming. I heard it but I was afraid to let it out.

While many people didn't know what they were supposed to be doing with their lives, I knew. Writing was the only thing that truly fulfilled me. Yet I woke up every morning and went to 'work' and by 9:30 p.m., when I could finally sit and have a moment's peace, I was too tired. Too tired to read, write, or even have fifteen minutes of quiet time, to connect with God. My work day took so much out of me that it left me with little or no time to be myself. I was too busy being an employee, wife, mother, friend, or whatever else required my attention.

I hated it. And I knew that I was a ticking time bomb and needed to get out. I wanted the freedom to write when inspiration hit, not scribble three lines on a post-it note and leave it in my bag for weeks—or sometimes months—because I could not find the time to sit and allow my thoughts to flow. Some meditations took weeks or months to take shape, while others could be fully written in an hour or less.

Sometimes, I had to make the decision to leave the chores behind and write instead. Unfortunately I am not as productive in the evening, so within half an hour, I'd be nodding off to sleep. Why I did this at 10:00 p.m. and not 10:00 a.m. was my choice. I followed a professional career, instead of what I truly felt passionate about.

But could I do something as drastic as quitting my job? Was that not irresponsible, knowing that the bills needed to be paid? Should I look to a less demanding career with more time to focus on my writing? Was it at all possible to strike a balance and fulfill my responsibilities to my creditors while serving my life's purpose? Did I not have faith that once I took the plunge, doors would open? That the bills would eventually get paid? That every area of my life would then be fulfilled? Should I quit fighting and finally surrender to the voice of my soul?

It took a few years, but I slowly listened to that still small voice. The pieces of my dream came together. Not exactly as I'd hoped, but if you're reading this book, then they did.

Life is short…when that small voice is screaming, listen!

#32
Intuition

Some time ago, I was doing some spring cleaning and found six unfinished meditations. I had not written for a few months, and it seemed like a great reason to stop procrastinating. I finally had the inspiration to pick up where I left off. I put the meditations aside with sincere intentions of completing them within the next week.

The next day, I read an article about paying attention to intuition—following the signs that show up in your daily life and paying attention to what life is telling you. Later that day, out of the blue, a close friend asked me why I had stopped writing. She said that my meditations helped her contemplate the meaning of life, and she needed them to arrive weekly so that it would force her to put things in perspective.

I was touched. But more than that, I knew that I needed no more signs. I made a commitment to write at least one meditation the next day.

I barely got to sunrise. At 5:00 a.m. the next morning, John Farnham was literally kicking me out of bed: "You're the voice, try and understand it. Make a noise and make it clear… You're not gonna sit in silence, You're not gonna live in fear…" screamed in my head like a speaker box.

"OK, OK," I said. "I hear you."

And just like that, at 5:30 one morning, I started writing again. And as soon as I started, it felt like I had never stopped. Inspiration poured in. I wrote four mediations that day. I also learned that I should not ignore the bold or subtle signs that yearn to give me insight on the direction of my life. I am so intrigued by where my intuition may actually lead that I have started an intuition diary. I record the little coincidences, the things that I am drawn to, or those that stand out of my *ordinary* day.

For now, the signs have been pointing to my laptop. I believe that if I really want to enjoy my life, I have to be in sync with it. Intuition allows me to do just that.

Life is short…listen to it!

#33
Maid to Do This!

I have a cousin who has been a housekeeper for more than twenty years. She has been chastised by her family for not pushing herself, for not furthering her education and doing something to make her life 'better', and for not getting a 'real' career. The truth is, she loves her job. She loves working alone. She loves the satisfaction of taking a dirty house and making it clean. She takes pride in knowing that she is helping a family who appreciates her skills. She is a maid and she is proud of it.

Many of us are guilty of forcing our self-development ideals on others. Not everyone is academically inclined. We are not all born to be managers, supervisors, or team leaders. Some people are content to be where they are. They like to stick with what they're good at. They are comfortable with their job and do not wish to complicate it. You may say that they are afraid to embrace change. And yes, for some that may be true. But there are others who genuinely enjoy their job, for the flexibility, isolation, ease, and lack of stress that it provides.

I know a woman who has worked as a receptionist for more than twenty years. She is the best receptionist I know. She always makes an impression. I can't imagine her doing anything else. It's her role in life. Fall into yours and let others be.

Life is short…allow others to live their dreams. And go live yours!

#34
Glimpse

In the movie *The Family Man*, Nicholas Cage gets a glimpse of what his life could have been had he changed one major decision in his early twenties. Compared to the life he currently lives, the life that could have been, seems much more fulfilling. Ironically, in the glimpse he also gets offered a position with the same company that he works with in his *real* life—although that offer came many years later. What is interesting is that he has ended up in the same physical place, but the journey was completely different. The experience of life was different.

When faced with a difficult decision, we all wish we could get a glimpse into the options. We think that if we know what lies ahead, we will enjoy a richer life. But can we ever know for sure?

I read an article about a young woman who ran into an old college friend. The friend was now married to a handsome man who worked on Wall Street and had two beautiful kids. The woman, on the other hand, was single and miserable. She was very resentful that her "friend," with a slutty past, who was not half as intelligent as she was, got exactly what she (the young woman) wanted out of life. Her friend did not deserve that life; she did. She was the one who played by the rules, never slept around, never got drunk, and went to church every Sunday. Where were her prize husband and kids?

But she and her friend chose different roads. They were probably both envious of each other without realizing it. Even if we feel that choosing a different path would have led us somewhere else, spiritually and emotionally it just may have led us to the same place we are now.

I may have mapped out what I thought my life would be like had I chosen a different path, but who's to say some other circumstances/incidents in my life would not have led me to the same lessons that I have learned so far?

It is easy for us to say that life for a battered wife would have been different, had she altered her choices in life. But if she were to go back to choose again, there could have also been some other tragic event or events that would have led to the same life lesson.

For a battered wife who survived an abusive relationship, the emotional strength and endurance gained from the abusive experience would perhaps also be gained from a continuous oppressive environment at work. But as a young woman, she *chose* the more exciting life with a wayward boyfriend instead of taking up a boring corporate job near home. In the first instance the 'battered wife' might have ignored the early and obvious warning signs of an abusive character, perhaps being captivated by his other attributes. If she were to go back and choose the job near home, she would be oblivious to the years of intimidation, sexual harassment and discrimination at the work place. Both hypothetical women will learn the same lessons.

You may argue that if we knew that different choices would lead to the same lesson, we would choose the 'less painful' journey but the very nature of our varied personalities tell us that this is not so. People make dangerous and damaging choices everyday knowing full well the harrowing consequences. And sometimes too, even seemingly safe choices turn out disastrous.

It may also be difficult to accept that such varied experiences could produce the same lesson, however, we cannot presume to know the impact of an experience on an individual. The thing is, whatever road you decide to travel, life will produce circumstances that will lead you to certain experiences, needed to propel you to your next level of wisdom.

In the movie *Sliding Doors*, we get a glimpse of what Gweneth Palthrow's life could have been had she not caught the train home. Again, the circumstances were different, but in both cases, the lessons and emotional experiences were the same: heartbreak, joy, major tragedy, and love.

Life is a collection of experiences based solely on the choices that we make every day. If you fear an experience, you will make a conscious decision not to have it. You will choose a different journey. In the end, you will always be exactly where you should be.

Life is short...you are right where you need to be. Enjoy the experience.

#35
Glimpse, Part 2 – Life Experience

Right after I wrote "Glimpse," a friend presented the opposite perspective. She believes that different experiences will produce different lessons as opposed to different experiences, same lesson. In other words, the lessons you experience in life will change if you change your choices.

We have agreed to disagree.

But through our differences, we both agree that it is the experiences of life that matter. If you accept your fate in life, wherever you are, and embrace the experience, it will lead you to a journey of self-discovery. The problem is that many of us reject certain experiences because we believe that we made a *wrong* choice.

Stop being remorseful about the choices you've made. They were *your* choices. Live with them, learn from them, and then choose again. You have the power to change your life every day. Stop blaming life! Whatever cards were originally dealt to you, remember: You hold the deck. How you play is up to you.

Life is short…experience it!

#36
Snippets of Hope

Have you ever been waiting for something that just won't come? You have this strong feeling that it is just around the corner, yet weeks go by, months, even years, and it still does not show up! And you search for signs, but somehow there are no arrows, no whispers, or light-bulb moments. All you have to lean on is faith. So you do.

Finally something happens and it looks like everything is coming together! But it doesn't. It is not the breakthrough you were expecting. It is just…hope. And soon you are filled with so many emotions: anger, frustration, fear, gratitude, joy… Yet the expectation of the birth of your dream grows stronger than ever!

That feeling is God dangling a carrot again because He realized that you were running out of hope. And you soon realize that your dream may not be fulfilled as soon as you expect, or in the form that you are expecting, but it will. Carrots are sent in the most unusual ways to keep you focused and reignite hope.

I swear, as I write this, "Don't Give Up" by Peter Gabriel and Kate Bush is coming through my speakers, and I am suddenly hearing it louder than my thoughts:

"You worry too much.

It's gonna be alright.

When times get rough, you can fall back on us.

Don't give up; I know you can make it

Don't give up; no reason to be ashamed.

Don't give up; we're proud of who you are.

Don't give up; you know it's never been easy.

Don't give up; 'cause I believe there's a place, there's a place where we belong."

The voice of hope is loud and clear. Listen!

Larry King once asked Oprah Winfrey if she could go back to speak to the person she was at twenty-five, what would she say to her? Oprah replied, "I'd say, hang in there... Hang in there."

Life is short...hang in there.

#37
Something Amazing!

On the final season of the *Oprah Winfrey Show*, Singer Jessica Simpson surprised a group of young girls with prom dresses and a new wardrobe. Just as they were recovering from that surprise, Dove, the skincare company, added a college scholarship. Overcome with emotion, one of the girls confessed that she never believed that something this amazing could have happened to someone like her. But Oprah reminded her that amazing things could happen to anyone, anywhere, at any time.

You deserve a miracle just as much as those girls did, and if you believe this, then you are more likely to receive one.

But instead of waiting for a miracle, give one. Do something amazing or unexpected for someone. You can go overboard if you are able to, or just make it a really cool surprise.

Change someone's life today.

Life is short…create a miracle!

#38

For It Is Written in the Stars

I know someone who can't go through the day without checking her horoscope. She even checks the sign compatibility of future dates and won't consider going out if they don't match!

I laugh it off because I know millions of us have no clue what the stars have in store for us, yet we go through life happy as pie. I also know that one of the reasons horoscopes actually come true is because we believe that they will.

So I decided to write my own horoscope. This past year I have spoken many things into my life, so why can't I do this on a daily basis? I can create the life I want every day. And whatever life throws at me, I need to stand my ground and remember what I am supposed to get out of the day.

I'm not sure if or how this will work, but I have been doing it for the past few weeks, and it's been amazing. There have been days when I wrote only two sentences in the morning, just letting them flow through me, and they manifested by afternoon. It's obvious that my soul knows exactly what it wants even when my mind doesn't. Mind you, there are many days that I am not so lucky. Nothing happens. But that won't stop me. I keep trying to be more in tune with my spirit and make things happen for myself.

I believe that we are more powerful than we imagine. I value the opportunity to write my own story. Some of it may already be written in the stars, but in the meantime, I will write my wandascope. I am the captain of my ship. I will steer it.

Life is short…write your own horoscope.

#39

Groundhog Day

I was listening to one of my favorite albums this morning, and though I'd played it several times, I was captivated by the soft calming notes of a particular song. I looked at the stereo, confused, trying to figure it out. What song was that? Why did I not recognize something that was supposed to be so familiar? I knew that I knew the song, but it felt like I was hearing it for the first time. I decided to let it play and appreciate its new meaning, to finally get the message that I had missed all those times before.

And just like it is in our own lives, we find ourselves smack in the middle of the same situation, several times…until one day, instead of getting frustrated with ourselves, rushing through it or looking for possible explanations, we just let it be. We open up to learning, and we are finally able to see things differently. The lesson unfolds. And we become grateful that we can finally move on.

Life is short…pay attention.

#40

For Those Who Suffer in Silence...

When you pray, pray for those who suffer in silence…

…For the millions who live in pain every day. Who wake up every morning with a wounded heart and go to bed hurt and alone.

…For those who try to mask their sadness by taking on the role of the characters that they or society deem suitable.

…For those who have accepted their debilitating physical pain as a way of life and are not even open to considering the possibility of an alternative.

…For those who stay in unfulfilling relationships, sacrificing their happiness for their children or social status.

…For those who have been marginalized and continue to be the subject of discrimination and harassment.

…For those who suffer various forms of abuse and are subject to extreme cruelty.

…For those who live with shame and regret because of circumstances that they had no control over.

…For those who have done things that they believe are unforgivable.

…For the disabled who are misunderstood and have no way of communicating their fears.

…For those who are lonely and afraid.

…For those who will read this and see themselves.

Though most of us will have brief periods of pain and loneliness, those who suffer in silence live in a constant space of fear. Fear for them becomes just as big if not bigger than the pain itself. And until the day that they are able to recognize this, we (on the outside) go on with our lives, interacting with theirs, unintentionally feeding the façade and not recognizing their pain.

Let us begin by offering our prayers for those who suffer in silence. Then let's start paying more attention to those around us, and eventually, we will be drawn to the people who need us.

Life is short…whatever causes you pain, release it.

#49
Find Inspiration!

A scientist sees the science in all things, while a comedian finds humor in the same. What is life saying to you?

Every day you are inspired to live your life's passion. I am inspired by the most simple and strangest things: something I see on television, a conversation, an emotion, my daughter, a thought. I can find inspiration everywhere—and so can you. The inspiration for *your* life's purpose is staring you in the face.

A chef, an artist, and a teacher could be standing in the same park, and each would draw inspiration from the same thing in different ways. A chef may see a blade of grass and get a creative idea for a garnish. I may see this blade of grass and be inspired to write about the wonders of nature. A teacher, on the other hand, may be inspired to give her kids an agricultural project.

Find Inspiration!

Our lives are filled with inspiration every day. Be more aware. If you are living your passion, use the inspiration around you to fuel it. If you are still clueless about what you should be doing, open your eyes to what is around you. You will be led to your life's passion and inspiration will find you.

Most thought leaders agree that the outcome of your life depends on how you *choose* to live it. Every day, life will give you various opportunities to capture joy. Don't ignore them.

Life is short…be inspired!

#42
Old Street

Diary Entry, November 1999

I seem to be in no hurry to get to Old Street; I've taken the longest route. And as I sit on the crowded train, I try not to stare. I want to write about the stories I see on different faces, so I pull out my note pad. Just then, as if sensing an opportunity to be in the spotlight, a dirty homeless man walks in.

He looks like he just stumbled out of the pub. He is shabbily dressed with no jacket. (It is six degrees outside). I shiver at the thought of homeless men and women on park benches and street corners.

He starts to ease himself into a seat and notices a fancy hat. He picks it up and asks the well-dressed lady next to him, "Is this yours, love?" She thanks him quickly and smiles.

Just as he relaxes into the seat, the train stops at the next station and a young woman walks into the carriage carrying a heavy bag, guiding her young son through the car. "Here, have my seat, love," the man says and ruffles the little boy's hair. "Hello, big fella!" The little boy answers with a big grin that gets everyone next to him giggling.

The man looks around and our eyes meet. He is ever so sweet and pleasant and gentle. And for the first time I notice that he is not drunk! And perhaps not even homeless. Maybe he's just lonely.

I look up at him, my eyes begging his forgiveness. He nods and his soft, sparkling eyes speak, not of pain, poverty, or judgment; only of love! He exudes kindness.

I feel ashamed of my thoughts but he sees right through me. "Cheers, love," he smiles. "Cheers, mate," I say and smile back at him. Through my clouded eyes, I notice the train pulling into Old Street. I am overwhelmed. I have just met an angel and I have to leave the train.

Life is short…judge not.

#43
Be a Samaritan

Last week, as I stood in line at the supermarket, I realized that the woman in front of me looked very uneasy offloading her basket. Tightly clutching about three or four low-denomination bills, she looked on nervously at the cash register as each item was scanned. Just before the last two items hit the scanner, I touched her shoulder and told her that I would pay for her groceries.

"Are you serious?" she asked.

"Yes," I said and told the cashier that it was OK to move on to scanning my items. At first the woman looked confused. But after a few seconds, she quickly picked up her bags and left as my groceries began to take up space at the end of the counter.

My first thought was, "Hang on a minute—she didn't even say 'Thank you!'" But then I knew that she was genuinely shocked and perhaps had no time to process what had just happened. Besides, that was not why I helped her. I was moved to. And whether she was grateful or not, I had wanted to.

As I was walking out of the supermarket, I spotted the woman standing outside.

"Hi," she said. "I just wanted to thank you. Do you know me?" She looked scared and confused.

"No, I do not know you," I said. "But it doesn't matter whether I know you or not."

"Then why did you do this for me? What is your name; where do you live?"

I laughed and tried to reassure her that this was not about me knowing who she was, or she knowing who I was. This was about me recognizing that she was in distress and helping her.

"You have no idea, miss, but God sent you." Her eyes started to well up. "I wanted to buy a pack of ketchup, but I knew I wouldn't have had enough money, and there were other things I needed that I couldn't buy."

"Well," I said, "now, you can go back in and pick them up!"

She looked at me, breathing heavily, and I knew she would have thrown her arms around me if we were not outside the supermarket. There was so much gratitude in her eyes. Then she started to complain that she had nothing to give in return.

"Please don't," I told her. I reminded her that this was not about her giving back to me. It was about her accepting what I had just done. And it was about her helping someone else in whatever way she could, whenever the opportunity presented itself – even someone she didn't know.

She squeezed my hand and ran back into the supermarket.

At that moment I almost cried. I felt like one of those Internet stories that you are not sure whether to believe or not. It felt really good. What I had done was second nature to me but meant the world to that woman. For me it was thirty dollars, but for her, it was another week of groceries and a life lesson.

That night, I was relaying the story to my mom and as I began explaining what happened, she cut me off. "Why didn't you pay for her groceries?" she asked.

"I did!" I told her and continued. As we spoke, she reminded me that I should never think twice about lending a hand to those in need. That whenever I could, whatever I could do, I just needed to do it.

She had repeated exactly what I had said to the woman. I had done exactly what my mother would have done. I had learned to give because I saw her do it her whole life. She inspired me to be generous. She inspired me to look beyond labels. The woman at the supermarket could have been a mean and inconsiderate person. It didn't matter. At that moment, she needed help and I was in a position to help her. She could have been me. I could have been her. I would have wanted someone to step in to help me too.

When Jesus said, "Love your neighbor as yourself," I believe He was talking about proximity—the one who is next to you (right now) who needs you. And whoever that may be—your family, your friends, your work colleagues, a stranger—reach out in love. Open up your heart. Give. Help. Empathize.

Life is short…be a Samaritan.

#44
Help Me!

At this very moment, someone needs you. Whether it is for physical, financial, emotional or spiritual help, someone is reaching out to you, and you may be oblivious to it.

Most people are too proud to ask anyway, so start by letting others know that you are available if they need you. And if you are the one in need, humble yourself enough and allow others to help you. Allow yourself to feel gratitude instead of embarrassment. Make the experience a pleasant one. Trust that someone is there to help you and not judge you. You are not perfect. Accept the moment for what it is: love in motion.

Life is short…we all need help sometimes.

#45
Health and Happiness

If you found out that you only had the next year to live, how would you plan that time? If instead you won the lottery tomorrow, what would your plan be for the next year?

As much as you may think the answers to these two questions are different, you may be surprised to find that the responses are very similar. People want to mend relationships, do more of what they love, help loved ones, take vacations, work less, take better care of themselves, and enjoy life more. Unlike winning the lottery, if you found out you only had twelve months to live, money matters would not be a priority. Extending the time you have left and enjoying life would.

And let's face it, ideally, that's what we all want: to have as many healthy years as possible to do the things we love. So, even without a big, life-changing event to inspire it, why not make health and happiness a priority for the rest of the year?

Resolve to mend broken relationships, do more of what you love, eat healthier, exercise more, take a vacation or staycation, and spend more time with loved ones. If you did these things anyway, whether you found out you only had one year to live, or won the lottery, your focus would most likely be on health and happiness rather than anything else.

Life is short...extend it! Take care of yourself.

#46
Go with the Flow!

If you really want to enjoy life, accept everything that it throws at you. Figure it out, learn to deal with it, laugh at it, use it...just don't fight it.

I believe that resisting life, rebelling and getting angry at it, stunts your growth. The difficult experiences will be much easier if you don't fight them. Accepting your experiences brings a calmness that helps you work through each moment and leads you to a deeper appreciation and understanding of life. You become grateful for the experience. You realize that something bigger is at play.

Circumstances change. They always do, however good or bad they are. So don't focus too much on what's happening now. Focus on yourself and how your life is changing as a result of your reaction to your circumstances. You will leave the circumstances behind, but you'll still need to enlighten your soul.

Life is short…feel your soul growing.

#47

It Takes You No Time to Get There

Diary Entry, December 2001

It is a moonlit night, or at least it's supposed to be. There are so many clouds in the sky, but somehow it's still bright. Most of the people around me are from my friend Tammy's office, but I am still very much at home. Eighties music is booming from the open Pajero I sit in, drowning the sound of the waves. Two guys have gone out to dive for lobsters, and we are well prepared. Next to the blazing bonfire, Tammy is bent over a makeshift grill, carefully scrutinizing the sausages.

My eyes dance around the group and I smile. This is nice. I am among friends and I am happy. I am motivated to write about this, so I use the inner light of the car to write on a napkin I find nearby. We are about five miles from the highway, at a secluded beach, with no cell phone reception and no bathroom.

I head for a short walk up the beach, breathing the salty air and loving the cold breeze on my cheeks. I return to find everyone slow dancing to "Sometimes When We Touch." It's like a scene from an eighties movie. It looks so harmonious: bodies swaying, heads moving, fingers snapping. I find a partner. We're all getting sucked into the atmosphere... I will never forget this. It's Friday, and after a stressful workweek, this is what we all need to unwind.

All it took us to escape were a few sausages, a grill, and some cold drinks—proving that some of the most memorable moments require the least effort.

Life is short...relax. It takes you no time to get there.

#48
Observe Yourself

Yesterday, I decided to observe myself.

I took a good look at *my body.* My skin and its composition; the roughness of my hands and feet and the contrasting smoothness of everywhere else; the full portrait of my face; my hair, my neck. I began to appreciate the function of every body part, from the quantity of eyelashes to the cushiness of my bum.

I took note of how I felt after a good night's sleep. I was very aware of the choices I made for breakfast and grateful that I had a choice. I appreciated the taste of herbs in my omelet, the bread, my spiced tea, and the fact that I was able to enjoy breakfast at all.

I observed *my reactions* to people and situations. I observed *my emotions* and what they physically did to my body. We require a certain level of energy to express every emotion, and it's amazing to observe our body's response to thought and emotion. I realized that when I got angry, my face would tense up, and as I yelled, I would feel it from my waist to my throat. On the contrary, when I smiled or got a pleasant feeling, my muscles would relax and I'd feel at ease.

I observed *my surroundings*. I observed my drive to work. The fact that I was in a car, built to protect me. I was aware that I was in traffic, writing on an old receipt. I was very aware that it was green and beautiful all around me. I observed the people: the homeless man digging through the garbage bin, the woman taking her child to school, the businessman in a suit driving a Mercedes. I observed the rain as it fell in one large sheet of single drops (amazing!). I observed a white bird perched on two power lines, unperturbed by the weather. He looked beautiful in the rain.

I observed *my thoughts* and realized that I was constantly drifting from observing my environment to something else: work, the collective consciousness. If we are all part of a collective consciousness, then who created this consciousness? Who created the laws that govern our universe—the law of attraction, the law of sowing and reaping, the law of intent, the law... I had to burst that bubble of thought and bring myself back to the present. I never realized how much thinking I did until I observed my thoughts. In my quest for the mind/ body/ soul connection, I was constantly praying and questioning. But it was really my observation of life that had led me to my new found awareness -The awareness of the mind/body/soul connection. The fact that I could observe myself thinking proved that my mind did the thinking and my soul was the observer of my thoughts.

I observed that this was a remarkable experience for me, and I felt compelled to write about it.

Life is short...observe it!

#49
Noise – The Sound of Silence

Many people are afraid of silence. The air has to be filled with something. For them, silence is a reminder that they are *alone*. So they fill the air with music, television, voices from their computer, their iPod, an instrument, or they look to socialize and run away from themselves.

I, on the other hand, *love* silence. And as Simon and Garfunkel rightly put it, silence does have a sound. But the sound or sounds that define silence are different around the world.

I remember the first time I traveled to Canada. It was my first time out of the Caribbean and the first time I did not hear crickets and frogs at night. It was extremely strange. I remember being in the apartment and listening to…nothing. It was a new kind of quiet. This silence was like a blank piano tone. On a small Caribbean island, in the daytime, silence equals the chirping of birds, the sound of the wind through the trees, or the lap of the waves in the ocean. In the evening when the television is off and everyone has gone to bed, silence becomes the sound of the night—crickets, frogs, insects, and the occasional crowing rooster. It's funny how this is silence for me, but my friend visiting from London found it impossible to sleep because there was too much *noise* outside.

Sometimes I lie awake at night listening to all these sounds and wonder what the crickets and frogs must be thinking. Perhaps it's finally silent for them. When I am home alone, I usually turn the TV off and do my chores in silence. I either get so consumed with my thoughts or so wrapped up in what I am doing that I hardly hear the hum of the fan, the swaying of the broom, or the sound of the washing machine.

External silence is more often than not silenced by our thoughts. When we listen to the voice in our head, we silence the world outside of us. Eventually, when we learn to silence our thoughts, we discover a different kind of silence: inner peace.

Life is short…creating silence on the outside is the first step to being silent on the inside.

#50
Listen...You Have All the Answers

While driving home sometime last week, my daughter began to complain that she was hungry. When we got home, she kept reminding me of the "burning hunger" in her stomach.

I asked her to shower while I prepared her dinner.

As soon as she got out of the shower she asked, "Mummy, is dinner ready yet?"

'Not quite' I answered.

It seemed like less than a minute later when she asked again, and then again, until I asked her to stop. I told her that I knew that she was hungry and I had heard her the first time. I assured her that I had prepared some porridge but it was not ready to be consumed because it was still hot and she would burn her tongue if she ate it right away. She would have to wait a few minutes.

'But Mummy' she persisted.

I continued to explain that she needed to be patient; that there was no need to keep asking when she knew that I had already prepared it. Asking would not make it ready any sooner. I understood that she was anxious but I also knew that she was not capable of consuming hot porridge. When I would eventually give it to her, it would be the right time and it would be perfect.

She gave in. "OK, Mummy."

By then, the porridge had cooled and was ready to eat.

Sometimes words come out of our mouths, and it feels like they were put there to ensure that we would hear them and give ourselves the message. God was speaking directly to me, through me. I needed to trust him. Everything I wanted would be given to me. I just needed to be patient. My dream would materialize in divine time.

You know, there is nothing like a real-life experience to explain a spiritual principle so clearly that you absolutely cannot doubt it.

Life is short…pay attention—you have all the answers.

#51
PMS!

This past year I have been suffering from PMS. During that time of the month, I am extremely moody, irritated, and hypersensitive. I began noticing that I was complaining a lot, I was super sensitive to all that was *wrong* in my life, and I did not seem to have it together at all. It seemed like PMS was actually giving voice to my inner self. So instead of dismissing it, I decided to listen to it and learn from it.

When I was younger, I used to think that PMS was something that women in their thirties used as an excuse to be mean. Now that I'm there, I understand. PMS just exposes a woman's true self. You see, in the twenty-two-odd days outside of PMS, women are guarded. We put on the 'wife suit,' the 'mom suit,' or the 'professional suit,' and we have no time to *feel*, so our real feelings get pushed aside and controlled, until the twenty-eighth day, when those feelings bust all barriers and let loose!

PMS helps women discover who they really are. Their defenses are down and they become most expressive at that time. It's like a truth serum. Some people say that they cry for no reason, but they are really crying for every reason—for all the times in the past month when they felt that they couldn't. They cry because they are overwhelmed. And they snap at their partner, kids, or anyone else unlucky enough to be within earshot because—let's face it—that's what we really want to do the other twenty-two days but are too worried about being a bad parent, losing our jobs, or offending our partners. PMS finally gives us an outlet.

Phew!

So I have learned not to dismiss my feelings during PMS, and instead I allow myself to feel. It's me. Unplugged. Bare. Free and out of control, bringing out the real issues. Unfortunately, once they are out, I have to face them. So I do. I talk them out, resolve them and then move on. Thank you PMS!

Life is short...let it out!

#52
I Need Emotion

Earlier this week, I felt overwhelmed. I just wanted to take my clothes off and scream!

If you've read *The Secret* or *The Law of Attraction*, you know that positive thinking and feeling good are the main catalysts to receiving all you want in life. But as much as you try, you can't keep feeling good every single moment of your life. Joy is not the only emotion. It must be ok to feel, to express all your feelings—whatever they are.

You can only get a true taste of life when you feel it. And every experience will ignite an emotion within us. We need to *feel* it. For instance, if you are hurt then allow yourself to feel hurt. If you are sad, express it. Cry if you need to. But stop suppressing your emotions and don't allow people to tell you what you should be feeling either. They are not you.

We all express our feelings differently. My expression of anger for example, may be different from yours. To get over my anger I may deep breathe or remain silent for a few minutes while someone else might lash out. Some of us move on from 'negative' emotions very quickly while others marinade in it.

I have found that finding 'positive' ways to channel 'negative' emotions, such as a punching a sand bag at the gym, or going for a long run helps them dissipate faster. Know that time is the only prescription you need. It may not work as fast as you may want it to, but it always works. Over *time*, the hurt, anger, sadness, loneliness or whatever you feel, will subside. And one thing I know for sure - the faster you allow yourself to feel, the faster you heal.

Observe how happy you are when you allow yourself to feel joy or any other 'positive' emotion. Notice that these feelings pass over time too. So embrace life for all that it brings. Remember that Barbara Streisand song from the eighties, "I Need Emotion"? Well, sometimes I need to laugh and sometimes I need to cry indeed!

Life is short...feel it!

#53
Word of Mouth

If you reveal your secrets to the wind, you should not blame the wind for revealing them to the trees. —Khalil Gibran

A few months ago, a friend (Friend A) betrayed my trust and really hurt me. I expressed my hurt to a mutual friend of ours (Friend B), who then went on to tell a friend of hers (Friend C) the same story that I had told her in confidence. Her friend, Friend C then went back to tell Friend A all of what I had said. I was totally unaware all of this had happened until Friend A ran into me and confessed how disappointed she was in me for letting other people into our private quarrels. For six months she had held it against me.

I felt so ashamed. This was one of those moments when I wanted the ground to open up and swallow me. It made me look like the town gossip. I had been caught red-handed and exposed. It was not intentional, but I had done it anyway. I felt sick. I just wanted to seek cover.

My friend looked at me quite calmly and told me that as much as she was disappointed, she also knew that I would not intentionally hurt her, so even though she had been cold with me, she was ready to put it behind us. I was forgiven. "Water under the bridge," she said with a wave of her hand. However, she cautioned me to beware of my confidants.

For the next few days, I was really troubled. I was very careful about what I said to *everybody*, and I made a point not to talk to anyone about anybody else. If I was having a conversation with someone, it was about the two of us. I did not bring anyone else into the conversation; neither did I allow the other person to.

My mind was working overtime. Before I said a word, I would be thinking of what I was about to say, whom I was saying it to, its potential for being misinterpreted, whether the person was likely to repeat it—I was going crazy. This consumed me. I could not have a real conversation.

I realized that most rumors begin with no malicious intent. We talk about people in general, we make reference to their situation, to where they work, and so on, and during that conversation someone may pick up on something and interpret it differently, or mention it to someone else not knowing that they are actually starting or spreading a rumor. Chinese whisper is very real and most times unintentional.

After I made peace with the fact that my words were not spoken out of malice, I was able to embrace the lesson. (That I should forgive rather than punish myself whenever my actions inadvertently harmed others.) Both my friend and I learned from that experience.

Life is short…in the words of gospel musician and author Kirk Franklin, "I won't harm you with words from my mouth. I love you. I need you to survive."

#54
More Than Words

You are the first person to hear the words coming out of your mouth. Choose them wisely. Words change lives. We can hurt or heal someone with the words we speak. Words have the ability to change our thought patterns and transform our personalities. When you realize that someone is listening to you, pay attention to the words that you say to them. Likewise, be very careful whose words you choose to listen to. They are shaping your life.

Words connect us. Great speeches have shaped history. The words of great men have created many cultural shifts. Martin Luther King, Adolph Hitler, Barack Obama—their words have rallied followers, and led different revolutions. They have all changed the world with the spoken word.

Be aware, too, that written words have just as much power as those spoken. You are reading the words that I write. In a sense, I am speaking words into your life. Whether you choose to believe me or not, I am having an impact.

Once spoken, words become more than just words. They become names, themes, ideas, dreams, stories. They have the power to manifest and become real. Our words create our lives, create history, and in essence, become our legacy.

Life is short...pay attention to what you say, who you listen to, and what you read. Words are powerful.

#55
Your Purpose

My daughter was only seven years old, when I asked her, "What do you think your purpose in life is?"

"Huh?" she asked. "What kind of question is that, Mummy?" She lifted her palms to the ceiling, rolled her eyes in a "duh" expression, and replied, "To be me."

Wow. With my mouth still open I gave her a tight squeeze. At seven, she knew that all she needed to be in life was herself. I knew then that my job was to keep reminding her of that. In about three or four years, she may lose that innocence and lose sight of her purpose.

She would soon be socialized into a world that defines a person by their career, wealth, looks and social status, among others. It is unfortunate that society is not interested in our purpose at all. We, are the ones who eventually define ourselves that way - usually after we fail to find fulfillment within the prescribed psychographics above.

Mind you, we knew it at seven. We knew that all we had to do was experience life simply by being our authentic selves. That's what our purpose is. Simply to experience life as an expression of our true selves. It blows me away that we knew it at seven. All we need to do now is get back to that place of innocence where we know that the only reason we are here, is to *be*. To experience ourselves through our talents, through the eyes of the ones we love, and through everything that is thrown at us. It is that simple.

Life is short...*be you!*

#56
Wisdom of the Ages

About a year after that incident with my daughter, she came to me one day complaining that she was bored. Then she began to cry. "I don't know what I am supposed to be doing with my life," she said. I laughed and told her that she was too young to be worrying about life; it would reveal itself to her in time. I reminded her of what she had told me many months before. She looked at me, a bit frustrated, and teary-eyed. "I know I'm supposed to be living my life as Kelci, but what does my life *mean* Mummy? What am I supposed to be *doing* with my life?"

I looked at my teary-eyed daughter, stumped. If one of my peers asked me this question, I could talk for hours about self-expression and purpose. It was a bit worrying yet interesting that I could also have this conversation with an eight-year-old.

While I wanted her to fully express herself, I also wanted her to enjoy her childhood.

But it dawned on me that perhaps for her, enjoying her childhood meant finding her passion now. Already she feels like she should be doing more with her life. I need to help her find out what it is and allow her to do it. Then her entire life will be one of purpose and self-expression.

Shortly after that conversation, I came across a website that asked the question "What does love mean to you and how do you express it?" Thinking aloud, I asked the question to myself. Kelci was sitting next to me and volunteered her own response: "I think love is a kind of force that I have to release to give happiness to the people that I care for."

I turned to her in amazement. I wrote it down. I was blown away. Man, I wish I was this insightful at eight! Or was I? Was this only my daughter or was this an example of how eight-year-olds think? Do we know how our children view the world? Do we ever ask them the burning questions? Do we think they're too naïve?

Although I did not believe that Kelci's response was completely accurate, I was nonetheless amazed at the depth of her thought process. Eventually, she will learn that happiness is not a tangible gift that you give to someone, but rather, an emotion that a person chooses to feel. You can release love and a person may choose to feel happiness as a result of your love (or not). But I agree that love is indeed a force that we need to release from our hearts to everyone and everything.

I have learned that children are so much more perceptive than we think. And they provide an interesting perspective on many of life's challenges. We should take heed. I have no doubt that if we begin the spiritual dialogue at an early age, with the right direction our children will be headed for an incredible future.

Life is short…the younger ones need to be heard. Let's start the conversation.

#57
Just around the Corner

About three years ago, I got this amazing feeling in my gut that the fulfillment of my dreams was just around the corner. It took about nine more months to move into my home, I got laid off, our finances changed, and through all the chaos, I still felt this overwhelming feeling that something grand was right around the corner for me. I just *knew* that it was.

A friend was, at the time, building his home, and we were toasting his achievements when I realized how far he'd come in three "short" years. He had moved on from an old relationship, started a new life, secured a coveted job, and built his own home.

I was so proud of him.

Upon reflection, I realized that for years, my dreams seemed just around the corner. Three years seemed like a pretty short time for my friend, but I hadn't even realized that the years had also rolled by on my end too. I had other dreams that were realized, dreams that I had not held to a time constraint. I had been so focused on the bigger dreams that I forgot to celebrate the other, smaller milestones.

Why do we place so much value on a block of time? Who said that *just around the corner* isn't five years away? What's wrong with five years anyway? Ten years after that, the five-year struggle towards achieving our dreams will only be a memory. We may barely remember it.

I trust the process—the evolution of things and the value of time. I have been visualizing my life and it is coming together.

Life is short…. Release the boundaries of time and just keep dreaming. Hang in there.

#58
Bad News?

I got a call from a friend some time ago who announced in a panic that he had "bad news."

I remember taking a deep breath and preparing for the worst. I will be honest with you, I cannot remember what came next, but whatever it was, it was not *bad news*. It was disappointing, but it was not *bad*.

I had to convince him that something good could come out of this seemingly bad situation. It was a bit worrying that he was so shaken up about something which to me was not life threatening at all.

A thing has no value except that which we give it. News is news. It is not good or bad. It is the state of affairs, the current situation. It's just news. We define it based on our perception of how it will affect our lives. A situation just *is*, until you give it meaning.

Disappointments are inevitable, but instead of labeling them, we should accept them as experiences that help us through our journey. Neal Donald Walsh said that "nothing is failure; everything advances you on your journey," and I believe that.

Good, bad, negative, positive—these are all words we use to shape our lives. Let us embrace every experience and enjoy life only for what it is.

Life is short… it is whatever we make it. So why not make it 'good'?

#59
Soul Budget

Yesterday, it seemed like my daughter was possessed by an IRS demon. She hit me with a barrage of questions about my earnings and demanded that I tell her how much I had earned in the last few years. I blurted out a figure, hoping to get her off my back. "Mummy," she said, "what in the world have you done with all that money?"

I looked at her, wondering how best to respond. "Well... actually, it's not as much as you think it is. The cost of living is high, but I guess I've paid the bills, bought food, sent you to school, bought the things we needed, cut the grass....' I drifted off. What on earth *had* I done with all the money? How much of it had I used to nourish my soul? How much had I truly enjoyed with my family? Or had I enjoyed at all?

You may argue that paying for food, shelter, transport, and utilities are necessities, but why do they always take priority over the other necessities in our lives? Aren't lifestyle accessories, body pampering, health care and spiritual enlightenment also necessities?

Lifestyle accessories are usually those things that we love - Pleasures that feed our soul such as music, retreats, books, meditation and time with our loved ones. Most times we barely squeeze them into our budget except when we feel sufficiently starved. Somehow we have convinced ourselves that the socially prescribed necessities are more important. And even if we are not extravagant with our lifestyle, these necessities always seem to suck up the bulk of our income.

But it's time to change the formula. How would the world change if we fed our souls first? If we focused more on our wellness and enlightenment? I was talking to a friend about this earlier, and we began to discuss small budgetary changes that could be made to live a more fulfilling life. It wasn't long before I realized that we had been on the phone for almost an hour. Not wanting to run up her long-distance bill, I started apologizing and saying my goodbyes. But she insisted on staying on the phone. "This is exactly what you were just talking about. This is what I should be spending my money on—connecting with my friends, not clothes."

And she stayed on for a further half hour.

How often do you feed your soul? How might your life change if you reprioritized it?

Life is short...budget to feed your soul.

#60
Life Coaching

About ten years ago, I met a woman who confessed that the key to controlling her weight and staying healthy was her weekly appointment with her nutritionist. "Surely, if you have the tools, you don't have to go every week," I argued. "Perhaps once a month to make sure you stay on track…" But she insisted that weekly visits were essential and that her nutritionist had one of the highest success rates. Her clients had been with her for years.

I can't remember what the fee was, but I remember it being high enough that my rough calculations had her nutritionist earning over a hundred thousand dollars a year. At the time, I seriously believed that the nutritionist was brainwashing her clients. Who needs to see a nutritionist every week?

Well, after a series of life improvements where I had direct assistance from a mentor, I realized that we all do. Anyone, who is committed to anything in life needs a mentor, a trainer, a coach, an expert…a qualified and experienced authority. You will find that you excel in all the areas of your life where you have a consistent coach. To stay in shape, follow the advice of a fitness trainer. To maintain a healthy lifestyle, subscribe to healthy eating newsletters and listen to food tips or get a nutritionist (I bow in shame). To achieve financial freedom, talk to a financial advisor, subscribe to money newsletters, listen to financial programs. To achieve spiritual clarity, feed your soul. Read insightful material. Learn about the laws of the universe, the theories and wisdoms that have been practiced for centuries. Search the web, watch documentaries, join groups, keep exploring, keep learning! You can find mentors and resources for every area of your life. Latch on; use them!

If you want to further your career, you upgrade your skills. Why should it be different with other areas of your life? I challenge you: If you want to be better at something, find a mentor, someone who will hold your hand and ensure you keep on learning. But be willing to reward them with payment for this assistance. Make it part of your soul budgeting. It'll be worth every cent.

Life is short…you need a coach!

#69
Committed

In January 2010, I weighed 153 pounds. That was my heaviest. I made a resolution to get back to my old weight—125 pounds—by my birthday. I got together with a few friends, and we committed to an exercise schedule. By my birthday, May 14th, I was 132 pounds, 7 pounds short of my goal. By then I had a whole new diet and lifestyle, and I actually enjoyed my routine. I could still be 125 for that birth year, I just needed to stay on course. So I plodded on for six more months, and one year after I made the resolution, the magic numbers 125 appeared on the scale. "Now I just need to keep this up till I'm sixty," I told myself, because it is my daughter's philosophy that "once you look young, you can never *be* old."

So I drew a line through my weight-loss goal and focused on a new one. That experience taught me that staying committed was one of the most important steps to achieving any goal. Achieving my goal was more important than achieving it within a certain timeframe. The journey mattered. Perusing goals change your life. For that challenge, not only did my weight change, but my eating habits and my lifestyle changed. Not to mention, there were also lots of small rewards along the way to keep me motivated. All I had to do was stay committed.

Life is short…remain committed to your passion.

#62
Write Your Bucket List

After I put up my New Year's resolution in January last year, I realized that it looked like a bucket list. The list of things to do for the year seemed like most of the things I wanted to do in my lifetime.

By May, I had crossed out quite a few of the items on the list, while some of the others were well on their way. Around July, I began to feel a bit nervous. If I did everything on my list, would I really kick the bucket? And if I lived past the year and crossed everything off my list...then what?

In August, I realized that I was leaning towards a career change. I had started my own business, but I also had other interests that I was finally free to explore—interests that would allow me to experience more of me. I was empting one bucket, but starting to fill up another.

126

If there was one thing I learned that year, it was to express myself without limits or hesitation. Procrastination will kill your dreams. If you want to do something, do it. I wrote my New Year's resolution on a dry erase board and had it stare me in the face all year. It was a board of self-fulfillment. And as I crossed things off, I felt a sense of achievement. I felt motivated to keep going. I was creating new experiences and loving them. I was literally making my dreams come true.

As the year drew to a close, I still had some unfinished business on the list. I transferred them to the next year's resolutions because I knew for sure then that I could create the life I wanted—by dreaming it, believing in it, and acting on it.

I do hope you take the time at the end of this year (or now) to write New Year's resolutions and actually act on them the following year. Resolve to change your life. Be proactive. Go for it. Remain committed. Make it happen for yourself. Just do what you've always wanted to. Live your dreams!

Life is short...don't just dream—wake up and live the dream!

#63
The Magic of the Holidays!

I turn eight every Christmas. I love buying presents, baking ham, seeing the excitement of the younger kids, running around in the Christmas rush, getting caught up in the buying frenzy. And I'm a huge fan of the usual joy and cheer that the season brings to so many of us.

No matter how physically and financially draining it gets, people always seem to put everything else aside and do their best to make Christmas merry. And why not? If we only do it once a year, then why not give someone a gift to show how much we appreciate them? Why not get together with family and share a meal? Why not drink a little too much and load up on ham, lapse on exercise and eat too much cake?

Most of us do not have the finances or energy to keep that momentum throughout the year, but we should try to recreate the joy that the holiday celebrations bring to our lives, at least quarterly.

At our family Christmas lunch in 2010, we realized that it was the first time in over fifteen years that all the family members were together. And as we exchanged gifts, I looked around and was reminded of a Thanksgiving ad from the supermarket chain Publix: "There's something about how each one brings its own special qualities, its own piece of the puzzle. So after all this time and all these years, you may ask, 'Is it still worth it?' Well, if all my years in this family have taught me anything, it's that when the right ingredients come together…it's magic!"

Life is short…enjoy the magic of the holidays year round.

#64
Soul Food

If you want to keep the spirit of joy and a sense of calm through-out your life, you need to surround yourself with peace and joy at all times—at home, during your commute, at your office, and at play. Listen to inspiring music, read spiritual literature, place inspiring quotes around your home or office, have deep insightful conversations with your peers, keep a desk calendar with a daily thought, and pray - be sure to connect with God every day.

Make your life a constant reminder of who you want to be. Spend time with those you think you can learn from. If it's not too late, reconnect with someone who changed your life. If he or she inspired you before, chances are there is still more to learn. There is always more to learn.

Keep feeding your soul. Once you do, calm and clarity will find their way in. When your soul is at peace, joy is constant. And to retain that, just keep feeding your soul.

Life is short…you need soul food.

#65
Calm

In trying to remain calm and be in harmony with all things, I make a point of avoiding situations that make me angry. But as positive as I may try to be, there are always some people who know exactly when to push my buttons and get me ticking! And we all know that sometimes, you step into a zone of negative emotion, like anger, and it takes more than a few hell-wrenching minutes before you can get out.

And because those triggers are everywhere, it is nearly impossible to keep our composure at all times. We sometimes try to hold it in until we get to a place where we feel safe, which unfortunately tends to be our home. And to release that tension, more often than not, we blow off steam on our unsuspecting, (most times) undeserving partners and children. Home is the one place we allow ourselves to be vulnerable. We usually forget the calm we held onto all day. But hey, we need to feel our emotions right?

Once, I took up a challenge not to complain for a week. (Not even in my head). By the second day, it had become hard. Really hard. But because anger usually precedes complaining, I was making a conscious effort to remain calm. Do you know that when you raise your voice, or tense up, it immediately affects your nerves and energy? Anger can make you physically sick. Your blood pumps faster, your jaw clenches, frown lines appear, adrenaline rushes, brain spins into overtime, and suddenly, like the Incredible Hulk, you morph into an unknown beast!

My mom used to count to ten. I never remember math when I'm angry, so I allow myself a few minutes to feel. Then, I breathe. I tune out of the moment. I remind myself that it really is only a moment and in the next, it will be in the past. I breathe. I remember that I am so much bigger than this; that this issue really is so insignificant, that I may not remember it tomorrow. I choose to remain calm, leave it behind, and move on to the next task, which is deliberately a happy one.

Life is short...maintain a calm temperament.

#66

Favor

When the right person finds favor with you, it can change your life. Many times people see potential in us that we don't see in ourselves. In the film *The Bone Collector*, a quadriplegic police detective played by Denzel Washington, having recognized the potential in a patrol cop played by Angelina Jolie, singles her out to lead a major crime investigation. After her initial resistance, she gets over her fear and easily slips into the role as if it were predestined.

Likewise, many people have moved up the ranks (in their jobs) because a leader saw their hidden potential and gave them an opportunity to shine.

If someone sees potential in you, don't dismiss it. It may awaken talents and lead you to new discoveries. If that person is in a position to help you succeed, accept the help. Similarly, if you are in a position to help someone achieve their goals, do not hesitate to do so.

Life is short...stay committed to excellence. You never know who's watching.

#67
Good Samaritans

It was the night of the 2008 US presidential election. I had just dropped my visiting friend off at her guesthouse and was relieved to be heading home. I knew Barack Obama would win. I wanted to be there. Well, by 'there' I mean in my living room, glued to the television.

I turned the car around and accelerated up the hill when I was suddenly blinded by bright lights. The road was not large enough to accommodate both vehicles, so I began to reverse downhill until I got to a place (halfway down the hill) where the road was large enough to accommodate the oncoming vehicle. As the vehicle inched past, I attempted to drive off, but my car began to skid. There were a few deep holes and a lot of gravel on the road, and I realized that every time I took my foot off the break, the car went slightly right and I rolled further back.

The vehicle that had just driven past stopped at the bottom of the hill and a woman came up to me to ask if I needed help. I was at an angle in the middle of a hill, stuck in a deep hole with gravel everywhere. She decided to go home to ask her husband for help.

Her husband came a few minutes later and tried to guide me, but the car kept skidding and soon it had slipped so far back that one of my tires was suspended over the roadside gutter. I called the owner of the guesthouse, who owned a pickup, to tow the car out, but he was fifteen minutes away. The man and his wife, Roy and Deborah, offered to stay with me till he came. I thanked them for their help but they brushed me off, complaining about the condition of the road. This could have been any one of them.

While we spoke, another vehicle came down the hill and attempted to help but decided that it was best to wait for the tow truck. As the two men and the woman tried to figure out another way to get me off the hill, a woman in a nearby house came out with a hurricane lamp and a flash light. We had been chatting in complete blackness for about ten minutes—there were no lights on the hill, and the lantern totally lit up the street!

My tow truck arrived a couple of minutes later, and when I was safely at the top of the hill, I could not stop thanking the five people who had left their homes after 9:00 p.m. (on one of the most historic nights of the century) to help a total stranger.

Driving back home, I was humbled and thankful. Strangers had literally come out of the woodwork to light a path and help me. And they were all good-natured, genuine people. Not once did I think that I could have been robbed, beaten, raped, or even killed—until someone pointed it out later. I assumed, as I rightly should have, that everyone who did stop genuinely wanted to help me. And they did.

Life is short…if you believe in the good in others, good will show up.

#68
Pay It Forward

If someone does something good for you, pay it forward. Do a good deed for someone else, then another, and as many as you are able to. Be an 'agent for change'. Introduce people to the concept of "Pay It Forward" by simply asking the person you helped to help someone else.

When someone helps you, help someone else. It's that simple. If you find yourself in a position to help someone, do it without question. And if you feel comfortable enough, just ask them to help someone else in whatever capacity they are able to.

Some time ago, I received an e-mail that asked me to tell one unsuspecting person that I love them. I found myself in a card store that day and was moved to purchase a card and put a monetary token inside to give to someone I encountered every morning who really helped set the tone for my day. The next day, I received a heartfelt e-mail about how much the note and the money meant to him. I was moved. This simple act had taught him that God had the power to use unsuspecting people to fulfill his needs. He also never realized that he touched the lives of so many people every day. It made him take a closer look at himself.

I never would have had that story to tell had someone not felt moved enough to share the original e-mail that I received. It got me thinking about ways in which I could show appreciation and I went through with it. I hope this meditation spurs you to action. You have the ability to touch someone. Do it today.

Life is short…when you receive a blessing, pay it forward.

#69

Be an Intercessor

Prayer is the most popular way of communicating with God. It's like having a most intimate conversation with a friend, spouse, parent, and life coach all in one. I use prayer to seek advice and project the most sincere intentions for myself and others. I know that when you wish good for others, you are also wishing good for yourself.

Praying for someone is sincerely asking God to assist him on your behalf. In other words, you're sending him good wishes. If you see anyone in crisis, pray for him. Before you judge someone, pray for him - and for yourself. Pray for those you work with, random people you meet (especially unpleasant ones) and loving people who touch you. Your prayers are powerful. And you may be the only prayer that someone's got.

Also, make a habit of praying for friends and family regularly. They always need it. Pray also for victims and family members recently affected by loss or tragedy. Prayers are positive energy support packages. And the good thing is that no one can reject them.

Life is short…remain in a constant state of prayer.

#70
Living Tribute

When Tim Russert—former NBC Washington Bureau Chief, moderator of *Meet the Press*, and political correspondent at NBC—died suddenly in June 2008, I felt an unusual sense of loss. I am a big fan of *The Today Show*, and in the months before his passing, Tim had been on the show almost every morning giving his views on the presidential primaries. He was always so excited. He always had a big wide smile on his face. He had been on the show only a few days before. I actually could not believe that he was dead. It was the first time that the death of a non-relative had touched me so deeply.

As the days went by, the tributes were the same. Although he was an outstanding journalist and an amazing husband and father, he also had genuine concern for his colleagues and their families and treated his friends like family. In addition, Tim never forgot his roots and was well loved by the people of his hometown. When you listened to the accolades from people of all ages and walks of life, you could only conclude that Tim Russert was a remarkable man.

But did Tim *know* how much he was loved? Why do we wait until people die to *remember* all the good things about them? Why don't we tell them or show them while they are alive? Do we assume they know? Do we just take it for granted and tell them if or when we feel necessary?

I vowed to reverse this trend. For a few weeks after Tim's death, I wrote to each of my friends individually and expressed candidly what I would say (or be thinking) about them if I were to attend their funeral. (I call this a *Living Tribute*) And I requested that they did the same for me. I wanted them to know what they meant to me, and I also wanted to know what impact I had on their lives.

It was a remarkable experience.

Life is short…start writing living tributes to all your loved ones.

#79

Love in Any Language

I wrote before about emotion, about expressing our feelings and accepting them as a part of who we are. Emotion is probably the only thing that we can all identify with. The poorest child in Africa smiles when she feels love, and the richest man in America cries when he is hurt. In the 1980s, with the song "Russians," Sting reminded us that the Russians love their children just as much as we do. And I bet there are angry people in Tibet too.

In every part of the world, our deepest desire is to receive love. When we try to connect with someone on a deeper level, the only emotion we seek is love. Sandi Patti sang, "Though our worlds are all unique, our hearts are still the same."

Life is short... Reach out in love today. It is the universal language.

#72
Hurricane

Diary Entry, October 31st, 2010

I'm standing at my window observing the hurricane: the movement of the trees, the sound of the wind, the raindrops hitting the window, the puddles increasing in size forming little ponds on the ground, the concrete houses standing still and strong, literally holding their ground as they resist the force of the wind. The trees are bending and swaying in unison, showing off their beauty and versatility as the wind conducts them to move. It's a marvelously choreographed production. I can't take my eyes off it. I notice the bright yellow stalk in the middle of a coconut tree leaf. The yellow is so striking through the green. And as all the leaves get thrown back, a bunch of yellow coconuts hangs out front. It looks like a peacock or large carnival costume. But then all the leaves get thrown forward and fold over the coconuts. Wow, this really is amazing.

I call my daughter to join me, but the whistling wind is a scary soundtrack, and as the power is still on, she would rather enjoy her silly TV program. My pen becomes my companion.

I am amazed at how strong and agile some trees are. While I know that many roofs will be blown off houses, seemingly weak trees stay firmly planted, dancing to the beat of the hurricane. I look for metaphors: Sometimes weak people can endure more than they think. But as a tree snaps and falls unto another tree, I am reminded that there are those who are indeed weak and cannot withstand the hurricanes of life. I watch the burden of the fallen tree cause the other tree to bend over. I smile. Another metaphor: Sometimes we have to support each other in times of crisis even if it brings us down too!

November 2nd

It has taken me two days to write again as I absorb the impact of the hurricane. When I stood at my window a few days ago, I had no idea of the death and destruction being caused in certain parts of the island. Moving at fifteen miles per hour, Hurricane Tomas took a full twenty-four hours to pass over, very slowly wreaking havoc in some parts of the island while entertaining in others.

As I learned the extent of the devastation, I wondered: If everything created is because of our collective energy, then is this how all our anger, rage and destructive thoughts manifest? I hope for our sake that our anger is spent.

So now, I turn to prayer, as we all do when these things happen. I am grateful that my family is safe. I'm appreciative of the little things, aware of my surroundings, concerned for my neighbors, and totally plugged in to my creator. Perhaps (I'm beginning to think) on some levels, I needed this reality check.

Life is short…prepared or not, the hurricanes will come.

#73

Aftermath

In the days following the storm I wrote about in "Hurricane," most islanders were forced to go back to basics. For five days I was without electricity. I used the stovetop to boil water and went back to reheating my food in the pots that they were cooked in. We played board games as a family in the late afternoon and laughed at old photos on evenings.

For fourteen days we were without water, and I learned how to take a shower with only a few liters. I cooked only two days a week. I grilled often so I would not dirty pots and pans. I realized how easy it was to use only my designated cup, glass, and cutlery for the day. And it actually wasn't difficult to keep the place tidy.

I drew closer to my neighbors. They pulled strings to get my electricity restored by the electricity company. We helped each other collect water from the rain. Bottled water was scarce, so I called them when I chanced upon some. We had each other's back. And now that it's all over, the sense of community remains.

I learned to swallow my pride and accept help from my friends. I learned to accept the kindness of strangers. And I learned that strangers are indeed kind. We received bottled water from my brother's Facebook friend in Saint Vincent. (She has never met him.) A family friend added thirty-six liters of water to his luggage and brought it over from a neighboring island. Another friend stuffed a barrel of essentials to ensure that whatever happened in the coming months, food would not be something I would be without.

Even though the Red Cross has classified some areas 'worst hit,' in some ways we were just as affected by the storm as everyone else. However, I realized that I have everything I need. Roads, taps, and power lines are all conveniences. I live in a good neighborhood. I am surrounded by great friends. It is easy to survive on little. And dirty dishes and dirty laundry means that even if there is no running water, there is food and more than enough to wear.

Already we have more than enough.

Life is short...thrive with whatever you've got.

#74
Aid!

I was a bit upset by the way the 'middle class' and others who were not "worst hit" by the 2010 hurricane were being viewed by the disaster organizations or those in a position to help. I ached for the single mother with a home and car but unable to make it to work. After losing two weeks' income she had no money to purchase water or other basic items; for the business owner living in a middle-class neighborhood, whose already struggling business got flooded and lost over one week's income but still had to pay his workers who came in to help; for all those who were cash-strapped and unable to purchase basic necessities, but because they had not lost their homes and did not live in one of the 'worst hit' areas, fell through the cracks. Many of these people were also too embarrassed to go to disaster organizations for fear of being turned away. But in the end, all of those who needed help eventually got it—just from different sources. The 'worst hit' got supplies from the disaster organizations, and the middle class got assistance from friends and family.

I know of a group overseas who had an opportunity to assist two affected families of the hurricane, but their manager insisted on sending the donations directly to the Red Cross because it was not their policy to help individuals. I felt sorry for the families, although I understood that with the high levels of fraud, this was a necessary precaution. Individuals, like you or me however, are not bound by such rules. In a crisis, if you identify a person who needs help, help him. Rules and policies don't always have a heart, but you do.

Life is short…in times of tragedy, reach out.

#75
Miracle Card

Diary Entry, December 2000

I stood at the bus stop with my hands buried in my pockets. It was freezing. Through my gloves I could feel the £1 coin at the bottom. I was deep in thought, prayer, and worry. If I used the £1 to pay for the bus, I would have no money to journey to the College to write my final exam in the morning. It was 10:30 in the evening, and I was the only one at the bus stop. I looked around and the night seemed to sparkle. Christmas decorations made everything look so joyful, making a mockery of what I felt inside. I released my scarf a bit. Even though it was cold, the air was crisp and fresh. I wanted to feel it.

I wanted to close my eyes and get lost in the moment. I kept fighting back the tears. I needed to write my exam tomorrow, but I also needed to get home tonight. People began to approach the bus stop, and for a fleeting second, I thought of asking one of them for help. But I might be perceived a beggar. I sighed deeply.

Very soon there were about six or seven people at the bus stop, and I was getting more anxious. The bus was due soon.

Someone tapped me on the shoulder.

"Excuse me, has the #92 bus passed yet?"

"No," I said. "That's the one I'm watching for. It should be here in a couple of minutes."

She smiled. She was a Middle Eastern woman who looked like that famous *National Geographic* cover shot. She smiled at me. "Are you going home?"

"Yes," I responded smiling.

"Well, you better pick up your card because that may be the bus in the distance."

"What card?" I asked.

She pointed to the bench. "Your travel card."

I looked at the bench. There was a "One Day Travel Card" sitting there waiting to be picked up. I looked at the woman. "That is not mine." I said slowly - each word spilling out of my mouth in shock.

"Well, it's not mine, and we're the closest to the bench so, you might as well have it."

I looked at her and the card in disbelief. I had been the only one at the bus stop for at least five minutes. There had been no card on that bench!

"This is the weirdest thing," I said. "I cannot believe I'm so lucky."

"Luck? You believe in *luck*?" she asked.

I smiled and thought best how to respond. I was not sure of her religion and how she would interpret what I was about to say. The bus rolled in then and saved me.

As we piled into the bus, I began to feel uneasy. Something was not right. I wanted to speak to the woman, but she was seated a few rows in front of me. The bus stopped at the train station and she got off. My eyes followed her out of the bus, and I turned as she went behind the bus to cross the street to the train station. The woman never made it to the other side of the street. I know for a fact that she walked to the side of the bus and turned towards the back. In the instant it took me to turn my head, she disappeared. There was no one on the other side of the street and no one next to the bus.

The bus pulled away and I just kept turning around searching for her. When the train station was out of sight, I sat down slowly and let it sink in. My prayers had been answered. An angel had brought me a travel card to get me home. I could write my final exam tomorrow. But more importantly, I had just met an angel. I was overwhelmed.

I almost missed my stop. I got off the bus and looked at the travel card. I said a prayer of deep gratitude, held it to my chest and placed it on the bus stop bench, hoping it could bring a miracle to someone else just as it had to me.

I paused, took a deep breath, and looked around at all the Christmas lights swaying in the trees. It finally felt like Christmas in my heart. I was so blessed. The angel was right. I was not lucky. I was blessed.

Life is short…expect miracles.

#76
Switching Gears

The recession of 2008 was similar to the aftermath of a hurricane. Everyone got hit. And after assessing the devastation, most people went back to basics.

When Everything Changes, Change Everything was bestselling author Neale Donald Walsch's advice, and it is applicable to any situation in your life. Financial management courses don't prepare you for a recession, but one can hit your family at any time. You need to be prepared to switch gears and still enjoy the same quality of life without the same quantity of stuff.

Recognize that what you used to do is no longer possible. Resort to a simpler life. You really can survive on less. Pace yourself: It's OK to give up the manicures but keep the hairdresser. Or you may have to give up both until your life situation improves. But once in a while, when you can, treat yourself to things you gave up.

Keep your dreams alive. Keep believing. Look for opportunities in strange places. Embrace this season of your life. Observe yourself through it. Learn from it. Don't be mad at life. Make good memories regardless.

Life is short...always enjoy the simple things.

#77
Coping

Without a steady income and my husband being away from home for over half a year, it seemed like I had a lot on my plate. A friend expressed concern that I had not come to her for support through my 'difficult time.' She was worried that I may have been putting up a brave face but crying myself to sleep at night. She was apologetic that she perhaps was not the friend that she was supposed to be because I had not come to her.

I knew that she was genuinely concerned but my mind wondered. Isn't it a 'difficult time' for all of us? Is there a prescribed way I'm supposed to behave in certain situations? And if I don't behave that way, does it automatically mean that I am suppressing my feelings? That I am in denial?

Is it possible that I really do view life differently, and don't subscribe to anybody's way of living but my own? Is it possible that in the face of adversity, I actually have the ability to remain calm?

A friend once told me that I need to recognize that my ability to be unfazed by life's crises is not normal. That my outlook on life is mine and not everybody else's. I need to recognize that it is a gift.

It has taken some time, but now, I do realize that I am different. Yes, I have this incredible ability to remain strong regardless of what is going on in my life. And, yes, *to me*, it seems simple. I'm not a fake. I just believe that there is too much to do in life. Why be angry at it? With a positive outlook things always seem to work out.

So here are some of the philosophies I use to keep me sane and level headed (and I honestly live my life to reflect this):

1. I love life. I am grateful that I am here. I am grateful that I can enjoy, create, share, grow, feel, contribute, and just be part of the process. I am grateful every day to have another opportunity to share myself. (I really am.)

2. I honestly believe that we grow with each experience. That whatever we are going through, however we perceive it, it is helping us to grow. It is strengthening our relationship with someone. It is preparing us for a greater experience. It is enriching our life. It is teaching us about ourselves. It is drawing us closer to God.

3. I embrace every experience for what it is—an experience. I surrender to it. I accept whatever challenge is thrown my way and make a friend of it. Being angry at life clouds my vision. I choose to hold it by the hand

instead, to go with the flow or ride the wave. It keeps my eyes wide open.

4. I focus on what's important: Connection—connection with God, family, friends, people and nature.

5. I find an outlet. With every experience, I write. I write about the joys, the pains, and the lessons. I share my life, so I always feel connected.

6. I bring joy to others, however I can, whenever I can—and I know that I always can.

7. I recognize that I am not the circumstances of my life. I am Wanda. Circumstances will come and go, but they cannot consume me because they are not me.

8. Yes sometimes a rough patch can seem like a football field. I lie on the grass and make angel wings, I roll in the mud, and for the most part, I run through the field and appreciate the space. There is a changing room somewhere out back. I'm heading for it! Things will change. They always do.

Challenge yourself to view life differently.

Life is short…this too shall pass.

#78
Me Day!

Every so often, take a day to feed your soul. Be alone with yourself. Connect with God. Rest. Laugh. Indulge. Do the things you love. Live in the moment. Just…*be*.

It may mean taking a day off work or booking a hotel room. But it is worth doing this as often as you can afford to—definitely on your birthday, and at least once every three months or even once a month if you're lucky. Make it non-negotiable though.

For me, a typical *Me Day* might include having a full breakfast, writing for at least two hours, taking an hour's rest, having a simple lunch, going for a massage, and relaxing to a great movie (usually a funny one). Other times, I have a movie day, a reading day, a writing day, a friend day, or a gourmet food day.

I believe in doing the things I love. I fit life in around them. And whenever I feel life taking over, I take time out, and little by little start enjoying life again.

Life is short…take time out for you.

#79
Fall in Love with You!

I am assuming you've been in love, at least once. And chances are you've probably gotten your heart broken at least once too. If you look back on these experiences (with whatever emotion), you will realize that they were all great teachers. And right now, whether you're in a relationship or not, whether you're happy or not, your experiences with love probably have a lot do with how you view life today.

But did you ever stop to love the one person always waiting for your love and attention? Have you ever loved…you?

Yes, *you*. Have you gotten to know yourself? Are you kind to yourself? Do you make special time for yourself? Do you treat yourself? Do you make yourself smile? Do you feel touched by the things you do because you know you're a good person? I am sure you've broken your own heart and disappointed yourself many times. Yet you keep on living with yourself.

Just for today, imagine you're your own partner. See yourself for who you truly are. Appreciate yourself. Treat yourself. Whisper sweet nothings to yourself. Do all the things for yourself that you would like done for you. Make yourself smile. Give yourself that warm feeling.

Life is short...fall in love with yourself.

#80
Introduction

"Tell me about yourself." It's the inevitable interview or date question. Pause for a moment and think about your answer. What is your immediate response? How long will you ramble on before you really introduce yourself? I have found that it is not necessary to talk about your family, background, or even work history. Most people are interested in *you*—your interests, passions, quirks, and peculiarities. So go ahead, give them a peek.

For instance, if I were at an interview, I may try to fit in the following; "Looks are deceiving. Though I have a very stern/businesslike appearance, I am quite jovial and witty. I love life and the various expressions of it—so much so that I write about my experiences in a weekly newsletter. (I might also add) Writing is my first love. I believe that I express myself better in writing than verbally, and for this reason: I function best in silence. However, I am also very sociable and quite capable of entertaining a crowd. I am one of eight children, so it may be easy to understand how I can be comfortable with both extremes."

I believe I have given the 'interviewer' a general glimpse of who I am. From what I've said, they can deduce that: I am bold and not afraid to take chances. I can function well within a team but can also work on my own. The podium is not my best friend. I may be able to write a report but not deliver the best impromptu speech. I probably had to fight for my dinner growing up, so I go after what I want in life and appreciate the value of what I have.

People can read between the fluff, and they can also learn a lot from the little that you say. Be honest.

Life is short…be excited to give a glimpse of your authentic self.

#89

Shame on You!

Why is it that people feel ashamed if they get dumped, laid off, cheated on, or cursed out in public? Why does the shame always fall on the *victim?* Or should I say, why does the *victim* allow herself to feel shame when she has done nothing wrong?

I have come to realize that shame is actually an emotion that we inject into ourselves. Society has led us to believe that *victims* need to be pitied to feel better when all this does is validate the shame that they felt in the first place. The actual person who should be ashamed hardly gets to enjoy any negative spotlight or shame at all. A woman who gets all her dirty laundry exposed in public by her ex-boyfriend for example, may now suffer from a ruined reputation and lose the respect of her peers. Most times, the boyfriend's disrespectful and shallow behavior is not even questioned. Public perception of him usually remains unchanged.

As a *victim*, I hardly feel shame anymore. I understand that whatever the situation, it is merely an experience to learn from.

Life is short…I am not ashamed.

#82

Bloom Where You're Planted

Diary Entry, October 2012

I've been out of full time employment for quite some time now and find myself in a strange place. Teaching Theatre Arts part time helps feed my artistic side, but I feel like if I don't publish my book soon I will go crazy. It's like I have been pregnant for years and I'm ready to burst! But I know for sure, that this is the last trimester. The last few months have taught me what I have known all along – That I am exactly where I need to be.

Unfortunately or fortunately, I was completely out of work during summer vacation, and my daughter absorbed a lot of my time. I also found myself being a full-time housewife for about three months. Having spent the last ten years climbing the corporate ladder, I was surprised to learn that being a housewife was not as glamorous as I thought it would be. There always seemed to be a hundred errands, I still had to struggle to find time for myself, I felt guilty if I didn't have dinner ready, and once again, my writing took a back seat.

However, I absolutely loved it! I loved running through the house after everyone was gone and getting the place tidied up. I was in a quiet and peaceful space. I *loved* the silence. It was great to actually have the time to do my chores. I was able to cook healthy meals and make packed lunches in the morning. I finally kept track of the bills because I paid them all at once and had time to sit and create a budget that we could stick to. I found that to get the bargains, I really needed more than twenty minutes at the grocery store, so my supermarket run jumped to at least an hour.

Some of my days were spent helping my sister with her new baby. Other days had me totally consumed with helping others fulfill their dreams, while some days brought me to my knees with housework. But every day was busy. I never felt unemployed, nor did I ever sit home watching television or wondering what to do.

As summer drew to a close and the new school year began, I was able to freely attend PTA meetings, pick up my daughter from school, and even plan a Christmas retreat. I realized that I was doing a lot more parenting, my husband and I became closer, and generally, my home was happier. We were a 'functional' family. I felt like I was getting a job done—one that I fell into but which was perfect for me. I was the CEO of my very own thriving corporation!

But...no one could know. I couldn't admit that I loved being a housewife to the world I came from. As an educated professional, it is almost embarrassing to be a 'stay-at-home mom' or 'housewife'. To put *pressure* on your husband and let him *support* you. It is *belittling* to fill your days with housework and errands. Admitting that you enjoy staying home makes you seem lazy and selfish.

But, it felt…it *feels* right to me. I *want* to be the one to take care of my home, to cook, to manage, to plan, and to be an emotionally available wife and mother. Am I wasting my potential? I don't think so. I am redirecting it. And with my daughter back at school, I can finally focus on publishing my book and creating a steady revenue stream. I am making a commitment, setting a date for this C-section and birthing my baby.

Life is such a great teacher if only you listen and allow yourself to be guided by your experiences. Nothing is beneath you. Every experience provides an opportunity for you to serve others and discover more of yourself. Welcome it.

Life is short…bloom where you're planted.

#83
Present

I attended a function recently and observed with amazement how the guest of honor always gave her full attention to anyone who spoke to her. She would stop whatever she was doing and make direct eye contact. There was an instant recognition of the other person's presence, a validation of his contribution, an absorption of the moment, a connecting energy—she was aware and totally present in his moment and hers.

So many things happen when we truly connect with someone. It's like a true moment of love: I acknowledge who you are. You have a voice. You are just as important as I am. I can't be critical of you because we are the same. I see you. I feel your presence as part of me. We are two souls connecting in this moment...

If we take the time to connect with others, to be truly present in every conversation and every event in our lives, the lessons will become so much clearer, relationships will be more meaningful, human behavior will make more sense, and life will be more enjoyable.

Start today by making eye contact with everyone you meet. It is said that the eyes are the window to the soul. As you absorb the moment, look lovingly into someone's eyes and connect with his soul.

Life is short...you have to be in it to live it. Stay present.

Namaste (The spirit within me, honors the spirit within you)

#84
The Wind of Change

My mom taught for thirty- two years as a primary school teacher before she retired in 2001. I would sometimes wonder how she feels having one of her former students attend to her at the hospital or service her vehicle. She was instrumental in their development.

For a brief time, I also taught five- to twelve-year-olds, and every time I walked into the classroom, I couldn't help thinking that they would be the leaders of tomorrow. And just like my mother probably did thirty years before me, I wondered if I could adequately prepare them.

This generation is miles ahead of us. They are learning faster, they are adapting at lightning speed, and because technology is advancing so rapidly, they expect life to deliver their dreams instantly too. As adults, we believe that children today are impatient, lazy, and unappreciative. New tech toys have taken the fun, physicality, and interaction out of life as we knew it. But I am sure my grandmother felt the same about cars and computers decades ago.

I drove across town one night listening to The Scorpions' "The Wind of Change," and I realized that each generation suffers the same infection: change. And the previous generation is terrified by the speed of change and the absence of virtue. In fact, many of them believe that it's the end of days. When paper scrolls were invented, I am willing to bet that the elders were upset that the younger generation did not write on the more permanent cave walls instead of paper. Likewise, my mom wonders why I don't write things down instead of typing it into a computer file that could easily be corrupted.

But as I cruised through the night, the words of the song touched my heart—"Take me to the magic of the moment on a glory night, where the children of tomorrow share their dream, with you and me"—I got a vision of myself as an old woman trying to understand the latest gadget of my granddaughter's time. I also thought of my grandmother and the people of her generation who are still in total amazement of what we can do today.

The children of tomorrow will "dream away in the wind of change" and create a life that they will adapt to and love, just like we did. And while it's OK for us to hold on to our values, I believe that we should allow ourselves to also be changed by the wind. It's the best way to stay in touch with the children of tomorrow.

Life is short…move with the wind of change.

#85
Over-stimulus!

These days it is easier than ever to feed our souls. With count-less self-help websites, podcasts, webinars, online courses, apps, e-books, and a bunch of free stuff—it's all at our fingertips. And boy do we grab it! We surf, listen, sign up, add, opt in, and download everything! We are hungry. We have an insatiable appetite for knowledge. We want to feed our souls, broaden our minds, and enlighten our spirit.

And we should.

But some of us need to slow down. If you are one of those always reading the latest self-help book, downloading the latest webinar, and checking out the latest app before you have even absorbed the last batch, you need to slooooow dowwwwn!

I believe that spiritual books are meant to be read one or two chapters at a time. As interesting as a book may be, try not to read through it in one sitting. Pause. Let the message sink in. Read the same chapter twice or go back and reread the entire book after you've finished. I can guarantee you it will reveal many insights that you missed in the first reading.

Remember, as much as you need to learn the principles of life, you also need to take the time to explore them and see how they apply to your daily life.

I love subscriptions that come weekly. I look forward to them. I get annoyed by subscriptions that arrive every day. These e-mails usually get caught up in the clutter of the forty or so others in my inbox and most times get deleted. I may only end up reading one once a week anyway. That said, I read meditations on a daily basis - the ones on my bedside table. I may not read a new one every day, though. Sometimes I read the same ones for a month before I move on. I want them to resonate with me. I need to feel comfortable that I got it. And as you know, I prefer a traditional book. For me, it is easier to bookmark the pages that move me, and better for scribbling my thoughts. Also, a traditional book is a physical reminder that I need to make time to feed my soul and unplug myself a bit.

So by all means, feed your soul. But don't get so caught up that you fail to discover the mystery of your own life. Don't surround yourself with positive quotes and inspirational material if they're only going to become wallpaper. Stop and read them. If a spiritual subscription no longer serves you, unsubscribe. Keep the focus on activities that nurture your spirit. Information overload is as ineffective as no stimulation at all.

Life is short…slow down. Focus. Manage your feed.

#86

Calm Down...Pray

Anytime I pause to pray, I realize that my demeanor changes. I am relaxed. My breathing slows. There is an aura of peace. I become a child...trusting, vulnerable, naked. I feel welcomed. I can be myself, bare my soul...I am safe.

I've realized that when we pray, we humble ourselves before God. We give Him our undivided attention. We speak in softer tones. We are deep, sincere, and emotional. We do and say things that we otherwise wouldn't. Even when we are aggressive and confrontational with God, we relinquish control. We recognize that He exists. We understand that we need to be connected to remain sane. And at that moment, we are humble and calm. We put aside our frustrations and pause long enough to be hopeful. Prayer is the first step to calm. After we pray, we are much more pleasant to be around.

Try injecting prayer into your day. You will lead a much more peaceful life.

Life is short…calm down. Pray!

#87
The Transition

Some time ago, T. D. Jakes delivered a sermon that gave me a remarkably clear perspective on death:

He describes a baby in his mother's womb—each month growing, changing, learning more, doing more, adding more parts and mastering his space. But while this is happening the baby also realizes that his world is closing in on him. He feels restricted and uncomfortable. He fears the end is near. And he is right. His sac suddenly bursts open and his body is being forced downward. It is excruciating. His head is splitting, pushing through a narrow passage by an incredible force! The pain is unbelievable and he thinks for sure he is dying. Then suddenly, there is a light, brighter than anything he has ever seen. He can barely open his eyes. He screams! He is still alive! And there are voices and joyous sounds welcoming him to Earth!

We survived our birth; don't you think we will survive our death? I don't know for sure what awaits beyond this life, but if birth teaches us anything, it's that a new life awaits after we die.

Life is short…but that's ok. There's another one waiting.

#88
Be Humble

As much as I thought I was being accepting of others, I recently realized that I expected more from people, based on the knowledge and maturity that I believed they had.

Many times, those of us who are a little more *enlightened* than others are not very tolerant of those who are still *worldly*. We forget that we were once in their shoes. We were once just as self-absorbed, we gossiped or at least encouraged it, partied, used excessive foul language, and lived without boundaries. We were cocky adults too.

Change did not happen overnight for us and it will not for them.

But know that your kind words and actions are enough to plant a seed. A friend recently told me that we all came from the same place; that everyone is loved by God and at some point or another was also loved by someone else here on earth. Even the beggar on the street was a baby who was loved by his mother.

But even if that beggar never felt love – because I do believe that there are some who have not had the pleasure of the experience of love – the little that I can do for him today may just touch his heart. If the recession of 2008 taught us anything, it was that our circumstances can change in an instant. Let's not live through our egos. If we are in a position of authority, we are there to help, not to criticize; to lead, not to be selfish or self-centered; to support, not to shun.

Be tolerant and accepting of others. Use every opportunity to learn, to teach, to be gracious, to help.

Life is short...be humble.

#89
We Are Family

When I was a child, the four-bedroom house my siblings and I grew up in was soon converted to six rooms to accommodate the growing family. There was my mom and dad, six brothers, one sister, our maid, two dogs, and the occasional roach and mouse. There was one bathroom, one TV, one stereo, and one phone line. There were no computers, iPods, or gaming consoles. There was a lot of screaming and shouting at bath time in the morning, and my parents had sole control of the TV (even before we had one with a remote). We pretty much enjoyed each other's music choices, so any radio station was fine.

My parents were very strict and made us believe that we were the only children who fought with each other, so we'd quickly make up because we didn't want to be weird kids. (How gullible you are when you are young and naïve!) We would play cricket in the street and Chinese Skip in the yard. We'd pitch marbles in my grandmother's balcony next door and play jacks with stones outside. And on evenings, we'd play paper games, watch parent-screened TV and then pillow fight ourselves to sleep.

We were brought up with Christian values, prayer, music, games and laughter. More than thirty years later, the infection continues. The laughter hasn't stopped, we still play games when we meet, and oh do we make music! We play it, sing it, and dig it! Prayer is in all our hearts, and though sometimes all of us stray from the family values we grew up with, the love that binds us together is still there.

Over the years I've realized that when we go out looking for friends, we are really looking to find family. To extend on the one that we have or to create the one we long for. Some of us are just lucky to have it the traditional way.

Life is short...as different and imperfect as they may be, appreciate your family.

#90
The Gift of Time

I remember one Friday in December a few years ago. I was sitting at my desk with countless messages in my inbox and a full "In" tray. My daughter's Christmas concert was at 4:00 p.m. that day. I had a press group arriving at 4:15. I had to catch up on the last two days that I was out of office, and I somehow just couldn't think clearly.

I knew I couldn't keep up. I had to slow down. Instead of trying to prove how efficient I was by doing too much, I needed to pace myself and enjoy each task or activity in my life. I needed to stop rushing. I needed to *take my time*. That was a light-bulb moment for me.

Time is yours to take and use as you wish. Time is precious. Time is the most important gift that you have. In fact, it is the foundation of your life. Time facilitates this journey. Time allows us to create memories. Time is a valuable diminishing resource. Use it wisely.

So with my newfound respect for time that year, I decided to give the gift of my time to my friends and family as a Christmas present. I committed at least one hour of my time to everyone on my gift list. I could not afford expensive presents, but I had time. And I used it the only way that all of us should: to create amazing memories.

Life is short…yet it is the longest thing you will ever do. Be careful how you pass the time.

#91
Create a Memory

"The holidays" should never be about how much a gift costs but what that gift means to the receiver and how giving it makes you feel. If you're giving out of obligation, it is probably best not to give at all. There are so many people who dread Christmas because of the perceived expense. They feel obligated to buy presents for their loved ones and especially the children in the family. Kids *expect* presents and they are harder to disappoint. But as much as they may ask for expensive toys, some simple inexpensive things can bring them joy too. And trust me, kids are much easier to please than adults.

If you give a gift that inspires, evokes laughter, starts a tradition, or creates a memory, then everyone gets caught up in the emotion of the exchange, and there is only joy. That's what it felt like for me on Christmas morning last year. Every one of us had a dramatic reaction to our present. Not because the present was expensive or exactly what we wanted, but because it was personal and genuine. We all felt loved.

I received an 'ihome' audio system for the kitchen so I would finally listen to the radio or my ipod while cooking without cranking up the volume of the living room stereo and disturbing the whole household. My daughter received a tennis racket which meant that she could finally get the lessons that she had been begging for. And my husband got guitar lessons from the music school. Until then, he had only played the guitar 'by ear'. These lessons gave him the opportunity to learn to read music.

Our gifts made us laugh, surprised us, and touched our hearts. We felt loved. And for the first time in a long time, we knew that this was a gift exchange we would remember for years to come.

When there is an outpouring of emotion during a gift exchange, you remember the gift. If you are gift-giving this year, give a gift from your heart, something that reflects who you are and something that you know will be appreciated. If not, don't give it. Your gift can be as simple as a breakfast delivery. On Boxing Day (the day after Christmas), between 6:00 and 7:00 a.m., what if you showed up at your best friend's doorstep with a Styrofoam cup of hot cocoa and a ham and egg sandwich? Wouldn't that create a lasting memory for both of you? You may even start a tradition.

This year, forget the usual bottle of wine or bath set. Give a piece of your soul. Connect with the true spirit of giving.

Life is short...create a memory this holiday season.

#92
Live with the Best Intentions

I believe that the key to peace of mind is always having the best and purest intentions—for yourself and everyone else. As discussed earlier in Meditation # 14 – Oneness, since we are not truly separate from each other all our intentions for ourselves and others, good or bad, will manifest one way or another in our own life. The laws of the world will respond to what you think and feel, not so much to what you actually do. Sometimes your actions may seem harsh, but your intentions are pure. Likewise, your actions may seem fair while you are acting with malicious intent. Karma responds to your intentions, not actions.

In the Bible, Jesus said that everything you do to others, you do to yourself. If your intention was to help someone and they ended up hurt, you should be able to free yourself from guilt because you acted with pure intentions. You can only take responsibility for your own thoughts and actions. Be at peace with that. Similarly, if you acted with good intentions yet ended up taking a fall yourself, do not become distraught or overwhelmed with disappointment. Remember that the law of Karma is still at play. Good will come back to you.

As much as possible, try to be conscious of your thoughts and live with the best intentions. This may mean making some big or small changes in your personal life and business. But it will eventually become second nature and you will become much less anxious about your decisions, and more at peace with the outcomes.

Life is short…live it with the best intentions.

#93
In Good Times and Bad

We usually look up to those who have gone through indescribable pain and suffering and admire their strength. Challenging times shatter our dreams and break us down, but they also build character, strengthen our spirit, and open our hearts. Many 'survivors' say, "I would not have been the person I am today had I not gone through that experience." And while I may be of a different opinion, (refer to meditations #15 and #34) I have great respect for people who have gone through adversity and have changed their lives for the better as a result. I am also grateful to those who share these experiences, impart their wisdom, and change the lives of others. I too am a different person because they went through that experience.

But while I agree that you learn and grow through challenging situations in life, there is also much to learn from success

190

and happiness. I have found that when my life is most abundant, I learn more about gratitude, love, family, sharing, joy, and peace. I am more appreciative of *everything*. I pray more, I give more, I think more of my passions, of connecting and sharing. I don't stop growing or learning. In fact, there is no difference. I learn just as much from the 'good' times in life as I do from the 'bad.'

Perhaps it is because the 'bad' times have brought me to a greater understanding and appreciation of joy, gratitude and abundance. And it is in the absence of 'bad' times that the 'good' times can truly exist. Often, contrast brings you clarity because without one, you cannot fully appreciate the experience of the other. So I fully open myself to the experiences that they both provide.

Life is short…in good times and bad, for richer or poorer, in sickness and in health, appreciate the lessons.

#94
Retention

Every time I read a book that resonates with me, I try my very best to live it. There's nothing like learning a new spiritual principle—exploring a new way of living, getting practical with new information, challenging yourself, pushing past what you thought were your limitations, and watching yourself change.

Like I've said before, I like to take my time when reading non-fiction books. I don't believe that you can benefit from educational material if you read it like you would a novel. It is not for your entertainment. It is for your enlightenment and retention. I can read a 150-page novel in a day, but it will take me a week to read a non-fiction book, longer if it's a good spiritual one. I want to absorb it. I want to experience what I'm reading while I'm reading it. I want to practice what I am *learning*.

While reading *The Four Agreements* by Don Miguel Ruiz, I was "impeccable with my word." Every time I was about to lie, exaggerate, judge, or speak with bad intent, there was a *loud* voice in my head: "BE IMPECCABLE WITH YOUR WORD!" It was so hard to stay true to this agreement.

The other agreements—"Don't take anything personally," "Don't make assumptions," and "Always do your best"—were a little easier for me, but during the two week period I took to read the book, I was *very much aware* of every situation that required my obedience to these agreements.

Then, after a few weeks, I became less and less aware until some new book fell onto my lap. As usual, I got fascinated by its teachings and my life got consumed with exploring that principle. Not that I forgot what I learned before, but when you're trying to integrate new information, it usually dominates.

About four months after I bought *The Four Agreements*, I lent it to a friend. When she returned it, I decided to read it again. This time around, it was so much clearer. There was a lot that I had missed the first time and some I had forgotten. I was grateful for the refresher. The principles were top of mind again and they were no longer a chore to implement. For some reason, it stuck.

On her stand-up routine *I'ma Be Me*, Wanda Sykes says that our minds are like a giant Etch A Sketch. We take in information, then we wipe it clean, ready to input new info, but we have no memory of what we just learned.

We want instant gratification in every area of our lives, including our spiritual development. Are we too hasty? When we were younger, we got textbooks for school. It took us a whole year to go through them. As the years went on, we got the succeeding volume or another book that built on and/or complimented what we first learned. Why do you think we haven't forgotten half of what we learned then? We took our time to learn it! There was constant application, practice, revision, exams...we learned using a slow, methodical, step-by-step process.

Why can't it be the same in our adult years? Aren't we building a spiritual foundation? How often do we retain and practice positive life changing principles? There's no point in immersing ourselves in knowledge if we are unable to recall it.

Life is short… perhaps it is time to go back to the old method of learning that supported the retention of information.

#95
Retention, Part 2 – Repetition

If this book has resonated with you and it has taken you less than two weeks to read, I would suggest that you read it again. Next time, read it as a daily meditation or take as much time as you need to reflect on each message before you move on to the next.

In our early childhood, we learned through repetition. Similarly, in our adult life, to remember something, we need to repeat the process until it resonates. After we learn it, we can successfully build on the foundation of the first instruction to grow in knowledge and become more intelligent, more skilled …wiser.

We all learn differently, though, so it is our job to observe how we retain information. I remember things best when I write them down. So when I read a book, I underline relevant points,

I note interesting pages at the back, and I make notes next to a thought-provoking paragraph or reference another book.

If I watch a documentary or online video, I make notes in my diary. Every so often, I flip through and read them. I also occasionally stop by my bookshelf and skim through the books that I've read. I read the bits that I underlined and the notes that I'd written. It saves me reading the entire book again, and it's a great short cut to keeping the information at the forefront of my mind.

I was fortunate enough to have had a good foundation in life and I don't want to forget it. Everything that I learn thereafter serves to reinforce that foundation. Everything I experience validates it. I now understand that retention is the key to wisdom.

Life is short…repetition aids retention.

#96
Seek Knowledge

As a child growing up, my siblings and I went to church. My parents ensured that we were well disciplined and adhered to common moral principles, and I think generally, I grew up a *decent* child. In my late teens, I began reading daily meditations, and by my early twenties, I was beginning to discover books and literature that made me realize that there was a whole new way of living out there, a group of people who live a life of clarity and meaning so much deeper than that of the ordinary man.

Such persons follow universal rather than social laws, they heed ancient wisdoms, they follow spiritual principles, they have immense respect for nature, they understand the concept of oneness, they believe in the power of love and they are always in touch with their soul.

Why then was I only finding out about this now? Why didn't I grow up with this knowledge? Why wasn't it taught as part of my school curriculum? Didn't my parents know about it? Were they and everyone else so consumed with traditional religion that they couldn't accept the possibility of anything else being true? Anything perhaps that would challenge the traditional beliefs that they had based their entire lives on? There seemed to be a lot of fear of opening up to a new way of thinking.

I remember looking at the copyright page of one of the books that I'd read and being shocked at the publication date—it was nearly a century ago. I felt like I had just discovered a secret by reading that book. But then again, it had been told a long time ago (yet somehow managed to be kept secret). Technology has helped to convey spiritual laws and principles to the masses, but wouldn't it have been better if we had known all of this when we were younger? I couldn't help thinking how different our lives could have been if we were socialized into a culture where elders used this knowledge to discipline and teach values.

It's not too late, though. The internet and social media, through globalization are spreading spiritual principles like wildfire. Books, courses and seminars are now all available at the click of a mouse. Cigarettes and Coca Cola were traded and transported in many parts of the world long before the phenomenon of globalization - Long before I was even born. In today's world, the knowledge that leads to enlightenment can be similarly disseminated—only faster!

Life is short…wisdom is out there. Seek it.

#97
Creative Expression

In 1999, I received a letter from a friend who was contemplating suicide. While writing a response, I found myself reaching deep into my soul, searching for the meaning of life. As naïve as I was then, I thought I understood it. It somehow made sense to me. And even though I knew that there was so much more I needed to learn, I also knew that life was something to enjoy, to embrace, and, yes, to endure sometimes, but not something to give up on.

My letter in response, turned into an affirmation of life which in essence became my first meditation. I realized then that I had something to share, I enjoyed sharing it, and I had an audience who was willing to listen. Plus, I felt a strange calling to do it.

As the years went by, I made a commitment to learning about life and writing about my experiences. Sharing my thoughts on life made me feel alive and validated my existence. I developed a hunger for insight, perception and awareness. I really started to listen to the wisdom of the elders. I discovered my intuition and allowed myself to be guided by it. I followed my heart. I did more of the things I enjoyed. I started to connect with life. I became well rounded and holistic. At times, I could actually feel myself maturing, growing up, getting wiser, calming down, and becoming the person that I'd always hoped to be.

And I owe it to this medium. It has provided me with a platform to express my creativity. It has forced me to be honest and to express my authentic self. I have found that constant and consistent expression, has enabled me to find clarity and positively impact the lives of others. Life makes more sense to me when I write it down.

Life is short...and it will only unveil its meaning through your creative expression. Find your gift. Life awaits.

#98
Pearls of wisdom

Because it's so easy for us to follow lists, I wanted to wrap up by offering few *pearls of wisdom*.
Here's to life!

1. Listen to your intuition.

2. Be authentic. Show people who you really are.

3. Express every emotion freely.

4. Live with the best intentions. It's the only way to keep a clear conscience.

5. Look for the answers to the questions *within* the questions you ask of life.

6. Learn from and live through the experiences of others.

7. Be a giving soul.

8. Enjoy the moment. Soak it all up. It's an extraordinary memory waiting to happen.

9. Be present. Make eye contact. Connect with everyone you meet.

10. Don't hold grudges. Love despite imperfections.

11. Read with a pencil. Take notes.

12. Get eight hours sleep every night. Sleeps repairs the body and keeps you looking younger. (It's my only beauty secret!)

13. Your goal in life should be: To be in a constant state of joy! Reside where your heart finds it.

14. Time is precious. Use it to do all of the above.

Life is short. Enjoy it!

#99

Pay It Forward, Part 2 – Be the Source

If you have been moved by this book, please share it. Pay it forward and purchase at least one more copy and give it to a friend or family member as a special gift. Post a review, recommend it to your facebook followers and tweet about it. This will not only help to create a community of likeminded people around you, but it will bring me one step closer to fulfilling my lifelong dream of becoming a bestselling author.

It is said that you need to be the source of that which you wish to accomplish. I have received so much love and clarity from sharing my thoughts with you. It is my hope that whatever you were able to take away from this book, you give it away also.

Life is short…glad to have shared it with you!

Acknowledgements

I am most grateful:

To God – For the gift of life and this life experience. Thank you for providing me with an intuitive mind and the wisdom to write this book. I feel most connected to you. There is no greater love.

To my husband Simon – Your unconditional love and support through this writing process has been amazing. You always seem to believe in me more than I believe in myself. You cheer louder than the rest. I love you.

To my daughter Kelci – Every day I am reminded that you are the future. I yearn for knowledge so that I can teach you. Yet more often than I'd like to admit, I find myself your student. You are wise beyond your years. Your wisdom, love for life and hunger for expression continues to fascinate me. I love you.

To my parents Emma and Sanders – For your extraordinary example. And for giving me the freedom to be myself. I love you.

To my loudest cheerleaders – Neil, Sarah, Nelson, Estelle, Deidrey, Jasmine, Dainea, Chadis, Keitha and Sophie - You have always believed in me. I love you.

To my editors Gregg and Estelle – Your comments were always right on point and your critical eye has made me more critical of my work. I am a better writer because of both of you. I've come to love you too.

To all whom I have crossed paths with. Every one of you, have in one way or another contributed to my understanding of life and enriched my life experience. It may not seem like it, but there is love in my heart for you.

And finally, to you the reader – Thank you for purchasing this book. I sincerely hope that it has opened up your world. And yes, I do love you too!

Visit me at www.wandaoctave.com and Like My Life Interpreted on Facebook. I'd love to connect with you.

Namaste.

Made in the USA
Columbia, SC
21 September 2020